A BRIEF HISTORY OF M

A BRIEF HISTORY OF MANKIND

A Concise Account of the Structure of Human History, and the
Features of its Five Main Levels

DESMOND COLLINS

Clayhanger Books

This book is dedicated to all those whose writings and thoughts have in any way contributed to the ideas set out here. I would like to offer my gratitude to all of them.

Published by Clayhanger Books
The Old Rectory
Clayhanger, Tiverton
Devon, EX16 7NY

British Library Cataloguing-in-Publication Data
Collins, D (Desmond Michael)
A Brief History of Mankind
1 Levels of cultural organisation
I Title

ISBN 0951131869

Printed in England by Intype (London) Ltd,
Elm Grove, Wimbledon, London SW19 4HE

CONTENTS

Colour plate I opposite

Barbed spear and harpoon heads of bone and antler. The three on the right are from
ice age Europe, while the larger one on the left is an ethnographic specimen from
Tierra del Fuego. By kind permission of the British Museum.
These are typical hunting weapons of the hunter-gatherer level.

Foreword

This is not a history of individual nations or states or tribes, still less of individual famous people. It is about mankind as a whole. We will be covering the entire period since mankind began (about two and a half million years ago), across the entire world and entire human species. This is possible because there were (I intend to show) five major levels of human cultural organisation, which each manifest a distinctive 'profile'. The history of humans is the sequence of the five levels, and I shall argue that every human community which occupies any of these levels has in some sense passed through all the levels which preceded that level.

The individual peculiarities of various communities and people, (interesting though they undoubtedly are), rarely have much relevance to the evolution of human culture as a whole. In describing each level, we will in essence be attempting to show how its profile contrasts with that of that of the preceding level or levels. In other words we are concerned with regularities or norms within each level, and contrasts between each level. Anything beyond this is not strictly part of human history, in the sense that the term is used here.

This book is for the general reader. The professional anthropologist or historian, who is interested in the ideas here, would be advised to read, first, two more academic books (Collins 1998; Collins 2000).

Colour plate II opposite

"Coalbrookdale by night" painted by Philip de Loutherbourg.   Reproduced by kind permission of the Science Museum.
This is the place where Abraham Darby and his successors developed the first industrial ironmaking processes, from 1709 onwards.

Chapter ONE   THE IDEA OF CULTURE LEVELS

The Five Major Levels of Cultural Organisation

Most of this work will be devoted to sketching the essential 'profile' of the five levels. But first we will briefly list these culture levels, before moving on to the criteria that mark the beginning and end of each one[1].

Level	Formal Name	Broad Description	Approximate Date of First Appearance
I	PALEORIC	Hunter-Gatherers	Two and a half million years ago
II	NEORIC	Tribal Farmers	Ten thousand years ago
III	GRAMORIC	Archaic Literate States	Five thousand years ago
IV	NOVARIC	Pioneer Rationality-based States (greco-roman and medieval civilisation)	550 B.C.
V	CENORIC	The Industrial Era (industrial and science-based nation-states)	1700 A.D.

Before the first culture level, there is a pre-human level (the Bioric, level 0). The members of this non-cultural level are probably best regarded as apes (or ape-men). Level I begins with true toolmaking[2], and is characterised by hunting and gathering. This level ends with the transition to farming[3]. Between each culture level is a transitional or intermediate 'interlevel'.

Level II begins when farming becomes the main basis of subsistence. It is the era of tribal farmers. This level ends when tribal society gives way to the state. Sometimes this coincides closely with the beginning of level III, but in other cases, there can be a prolonged interval[4]. Level III begins with literacy and the use of a formal script. It is the era of archaic (pre-classical or non-classical) civilisations. This level ends with the introduction of a vowelled phonetic script[5].

Level IV begins when a vowelled phonetic alphabet is joined by a tradition of rational thought. It encompasses the greco-roman and 'medieval' eras. Level IV ends with the dawn of the scientific revolution about 1500 A.D. Level V, the industrial era, begins with the dawn of the industrial revolution at about 1700 A.D. (No definition of its close has yet been fixed.)

The reader who wishes to get straight on with the narrative is invited to move directly to chapter two.

The General Theory of Culture Levels [6]

We can now review the main underlying principles on which the general theory is based. There are two preliminaries. The first is to settle on a scheme which is thought adequate for the purpose, as we have done above. The second is to note that the system will only work, and can only be usefully evaluated, if the levels are formally and precisely defined. Informal terms, like tribal farmers or hunter-gatherers, in reality stand for more formal terms, which have a very precise meaning. (Words like civilisation, hunters and even industry and science have been used in vague or extended senses, which can be quite misleading). With this proviso, everyday terms are used regularly in this work in the hope of making it more user-friendly.

The five main levels of culture have not been selected simply as a convenient way to present human history, (though I hope they do serve this purpose quite well). There are also more serious claims made on behalf of the scheme of culture levels. The first of these principles concerns *'necessary sequence'* – the idea that for mankind to reach the later or higher levels[7], it is necessary for mankind (in part at least) to have passed through the previous or lower levels.

All this would be quite straightforward were we to confine our attention to a group of societies which all started at the same level (say level I). It is possible for such societies to make the transition to the next level (II in this case), and achieve a stable adaptation at the new level (given a little time); this is known to have happened many times in the past. The principle of necessary sequence asserts that it is not possible for such societies to make the transition direct to the next but one level (level III in this case), still less to any of the higher levels (IV or V)[8]. Thus we are saying that by-passing or 'leap-frogging' levels cannot occur[9].

Complication arises because societies do not necessarily move to higher levels at the same pace, or even at all. There are a variety of reasons for this (such as that in an area with no plants suitable for cultivation, hunters could not make the transition to farming), but we do not need to pursue these here. As a result it is quite common for a society to come into contact with another society at a higher level. Indeed one of the commonest reasons for moving to the next level is such contact (which, as we shall see under the fourth principle below, is often called acculturation). But independent advance definitely also happens.

In a situation where a society comes into contact with a second society, which is not just one, but two or more, levels higher, one might expect that the lower society would still be acculturated, and would move two or more levels upward. This would not of course be a case of independent 'leap-frogging', because the society in question would have passed, by proxy as it were, through any missing levels. Such assisted leap-frogging, leading to a new stable adaptation, is extremely rare, if it exists at all. It is commoner for lower level societies to collapse, or be absorbed, under these circumstances, by conquest or otherwise. A few individuals may make the transition, or more likely a few of their half-breed progeny will. Successful leap-frogging of levels I and II has rarely, or never as far as I know, been possible in the past; however by-passing of levels III and IV has (though rare and always as a result of massive acculturation) apparently happened[10], and was evidently somewhat less difficult than for the previous levels.

A second major principle is *directionality*. The levels are numbered from I to V because that is the direction which cultural evolution evidently takes. There is ample archaeological and historical evidence that all tribal farmers were preceded by hunter-gatherers; that all states were preceded by tribal farmers; and that 'archaic' states precede the dawn of 'rationality', and the industrial era. Furthermore there are good theoretical reasons why one would expect cultural evolution to occur in this direction, rather than randomly or in the reverse direction. We shall meet in the succeeding chapters several clear examples of directionality, such as population density; life expectancy; and *per capita* wealth.

Are we saying that it is impossible for a society of one level to move or 'evolve' to a lower level? It is not quite as simple as this. Small numbers of individuals or groups may be forced or required by circumstances to abandon some of the cultural features typical of their level[11]. When such apparent reversions have occurred, it turns out that the 'reverters' do not in fact move to the same kind of stable adaptation that had formerly characterised the level below. They usually exhibit an uneasy mixture of the two levels[12]. Reverting to a lower level and re-achieving a stable adaptation to that level does not apparently occur, and there are usually good practical reasons why this is not feasible; the markedly higher density of population in higher levels, for example, usually militates against it.

Before going on to any further principles, it is necessary to make an important clarification; this is the principle of *objectivity*. It cannot be too strongly emphasised that the theory and scheme of culture levels, and their evaluation, do not involve moral or value judgements, nor even aesthetic judgements. It may not be possible to discourage people from making value judgements about historical facts and theories, but such judgements have no bearing on the truth or falsehood of the theories or supposed facts themselves. The factual claims about culture levels are either objectively true or objectively false. A phenomenon like increased average longevity is not a value judgement, (though of course most people would want to make a value judgement about its desirability). It is no more 'eurocentric' to research longevity or the sequence of culture levels, than it is to research nuclear physics or dinosaurs; in a sense, all objective research is 'eurocentric'. The theory of culture levels is concerned with factual questions, not moral questions. No amount of research into the facts of history ever logically entails a moral judgement about those facts[13], just as moral judgements never have any logical bearing on the truth of such facts.

The scheme of culture levels does not imply any 'law of inevitability'. The fact that we learn a lot about cultural 'progress', or even why it occurs, does not in any way indicate that such progress is inevitable. The reader may well take the view that at the current industrial level, further technological advance is virtually unstoppable, but this would only be so provided that certain basic conditions applied, and we have no right to regard these as given. Both internal and external catastrophes could end technological progress.

(An obvious example of an internal factor would be a nuclear war which destroyed all industrial peoples; and an external catastrophe might be a giant meteorite, which destroyed human life.)

For just these kind of reasons, reliable and accurate predictions of the future cannot be made. Assuming a series of likely conditions, we might be lucky enough to guess some of the developments the future holds, but we cannot say they are inevitable.

A fourth principle concerns *acculturation* (the effect of which we have already noted in connection with necessary sequence). Without acculturation, as we have noted, the progress through the culture levels, if and when it occurred, would be relatively straightforward. But in the real world, acculturation between societies, both at the same level and at different levels, is likely to occur often. Societies which have been acculturated from a higher culture level, but have not fully achieved that level, are most appropriately placed in the interlevel between the two (see below).

When culture contact occurs between two peoples, the transference of ideas will often be in both directions. But when a higher level society impinges on a lower level society, the movement of techniques and ideas is much greater from the higher to the lower level. This constitutes an extra sub-principle of 'higher level culture dominance'. Higher culture level societies regularly incorporate or destroy lower level societies.

For a full picture of the cultural status of human societies in general, according to the model we are proposing, it is necessary to have a *complete culture scheme*. We have already noted a pre-human level, and the five main culture levels. (There are also valid sub-levels in these levels, which mankind as a whole could not bypass[14], but for our present purposes it is not necessary to go into the details of these here.) Between the five culture levels, there are in each case *interlevels*. They include societies which are transitional from one level to the next, but also societies which are intermediate for other reasons. For example, whole tribes of nomadic pastoralists, who have no products from cultivation, are intermediate between levels I and II. In addition the acculturation between societies which are at different levels often results in culture which is intermediate.[15]

A sixth principle follows from the above. If the theory is correct, all human societies belong either to one of the five levels or to an interlevel. (The latter includes, as we saw above, transitional, intermediate and acculturated peoples.) In other words certain notional kinds of society, (for example true hunter-gatherers, possessing advanced experimental science or nuclear technology), are predicted to be impossible, and not to exist. This is the principle of *inclusiveness*.

A further principle is that all societies, which belong to a particular level, regularly exhibit a 'profile' or set of similarities across a wide range from technological and economic features, through social and political, to sectors like communication and thought. On closer inspection these features are often found to be linked by *interconn-ections*, though rarely in a directly causal way.

The last principle need not detain us long. It notes simply that those societies, in which interaction and openness are normal, tend to be more successful at innovation and 'progress'. Conversely those which isolate themselves, and discourage open or critical discussion and thought, tend to perform poorly in this respect.

A brief look at how this research has been pursued follows. All research consciously or unconsciously uses a theory of knowledge, or of how we 'learn'. The view followed is quite explicit. All knowledge begins with conjecture, and proceeds by trial and error[16]. So long as the theories can be tested or evaluated in some rational or factual way, we can form a judgement on whether they stand up to testing. If they do, then they are to some extent corroborated, and are close to the truth in this way. We select those which stand up best to evaluation.

Since our purpose here is to search for generalisations concerning human history, it is quite natural that we should try to follow essentially the same underlying method as is used in the natural sciences, (where generalisations or theories, on as large a scale as possible, are sought and evaluated).

The generalisations which are easiest to test are those which can claim to have no exceptions; (in other words, they are true 'universals'). Even in the natural sciences, true universals are not easy to find. There are apparently some universals in culture levels (as we shall see below), but more often we come across what seem to be near-universals or 'norms'. These are less easy to test satisfactorily, but they can still be objectively evaluated. Often one suspects that the rare exceptions are due to faulty or misleading data[17].

The evidence considered in choosing and defining the levels of culture is diverse. Written or historical sources are available only for the last three levels, (and even here it is very thin for level III, and only good for level V). Archaeological evidence (often crucially aided by dating techniques from the natural sciences) can be extremely valuable across all the levels. It is useful on questions of the broad time scale, and also in areas like technology. However, on a whole range of questions to do with social and political organisation, thought and religion, it is of very limited value.

For the first two levels of culture, much of the most useful evidence comes from 'primitive' peoples who were studied in recent centuries, when they were still at levels I and II; (this is ethnographic or anthropological evidence). Other sources (such as fossil remains of apes and other primates, and developmental psychology) need to be considered, especially for the pre-human level, where studies of ape behaviour and relevant fossils can be important. A list of the main cases of hunter-gatherers and tribal farmers, for which we have useful evidence, will be found in appendix A, along with a list of the main relevant literate states of levels III, IV and V.

One last point concerning method is that generalisations about levels should never be made on the basis of a single example, when there exists a number or range of available cases. Evaluation of the theories set out here should obviously always employ the widest range of relevant evidence possible.

Chapter TWO   THE LEVEL OF PRE-HUMAN ANCESTORS: Level 0 (the Bioric)

There is widespread agreement among researchers on human evolution that the ancestors of humans parted company from the ancestors of chimpanzees in the miocene period; before that they were a single lineage. There is little doubt that the common ancestor of these two lineages lived in Africa, as Darwin first pointed out in 1871. The last common ancestor, before the separation of the lineages occurred, is currently thought to have lived about six million years ago, near the end of the miocene period. (This figure is based on an interpretation of the molecular evidence and should be seen as provisional. Fossil evidence seems to rule out a date later than about five million years ago, but an earlier date would seem to be possible on fossil evidence.)

The only practical definition for the beginning of 'humans' is the appearance of stone tool making. Because stone tools are virtually indestructible, archaeologists (usually in collaboration with geologists) should be able to determine when stone tool making first begins. The answer seems to be that it was close to two and a half million years ago; and the fact that, for a long time after this date, stone tools are only reliably known from Africa, strengthens the case for an african origin of both humans and stone tool making[1].

There are thus two relatively recent phases in the pre-human ancestry of humans (as defined above), namely between the last common ancestor and the first toolmaking humans (about six to two and a half million years ago) - and before this the common ancestor of chimps and humans (in the several million years before about six million years ago). We may now examine these two stages in our pre-human ancestry.

The ape-human common ancestor

The common ancestor probably looked much like a chimpanzee, and the obvious exemplar for constructing a broad picture of its behaviour is the chimpanzee, of which two species survive. The food supply presumably came from foraging. It probably encompassed the same broad range of foods that are still eaten by chimps. This is primarily vegetation, especially fruits, nuts, leaves and shoots; secondly insects and other very small creatures; and lastly, but significantly, occasional food from small mammals, such as bushbuck, monkeys and bushpig; (but these latter mammals provide very small amounts of food compared to the other sources[2]). Chimpanzees, and other 'herbivores' eat a considerably greater bulk of food, compared to humans, because of the generally lower nutritional value of their food for tissue replacement.

Toolusing is found in common chimps. There have been four main kinds reported. Stalks or twigs are poked into anthills to 'fish for' termites; stones or wooden blocks are used to crack nuts; vegetation is chewed into a mush to use as a sponge for soaking up water; and leaves are used as 'wipes'. Toolusing is found among several widely differing vertebrates, for example in finches and sea otters. Toolmaking, of the sort found in even the most primitive humans, is not found in chimps, and even the toolusing is apparently unknown in the 'pygmy' chimp or bonobo. Therefore it seems either toolusing has been lost by bonobos, or more likely it did not exist more than about six million years ago in the common ancestor, before bonobos and human ancestors had parted company. If there was toolusing in the common ancestral population, I would assume that it was only of the most simple kind.

Chimpanzees belong to loose communities or troops, and something similar seems plausible for the common ancestor. In neither species of chimpanzee, nor in the gorillas, do we find that the male who fathers an offspring, and the female who bears it, remain together to rear the child or form a family. Also these three species, like, most primates, are hierarchical rather than egalitarian. Position in the male hierarchy in general determines first or privileged access to the females. But it also carries the obligation to defend the group and to lead its members to their successive feeding grounds. Progress in the hierarchy tends to depend on physical prowess or the formation of alliances (sometimes called 'chimpanzee politics'). All these features are likely to have existed in the common ancestral population. The idea of a marriage custom, or the recognition of kinship relations across generations between males can almost certainly be ruled out at this level. Apes are not especially violent or murderous, but neither are they paragons of peacefulness and restraint. Fighting and killing do occur[3], and no doubt did in the common ancestral population.

Chimpanzees do not have speech, so it is reasonably certain that the common ancestor also lacked it[4]. However, many primates do have a call system, and the sort of 'calls' found in chimpanzees are likely to have been present in the common ancestor. Some communication is also possible through facial expression, but we should not expect anything more complicated than is present in our closest cousin species.

There is reason to believe that chimpanzee thought is analogous to that of modern children of about two years of age[5]. They seem to be capable of such things as deferred imitation, 'symbolic' play, pretence and even deception, and they may have a modest capacity for 'insight'. (Some workers have considered that insight is indicated by chimps who fetch a box to enable them to get up to a banana, suspended out of reach; in captivity they even pile one box on top of another – apparently with little trial and error beforehand.) The common 'chimp-human' ancestor may be expected to have had a similar level of thought to the apes.

Pre-humans since the common ancestor

A large number of fossils relevant to pre-human ancestry have been found in Africa from the early and middle pliocene (in the period six to two and a half million years ago). They are formally classified as 'Hominidae' or hominids, meaning members of the 'family' or branch to which humans belong; (but there are no known fossils of the chimp branch). Most of these hominids have been broadly grouped as gracile *Australopithecus* (or gracile australopithecines). Some authorities insist that there are many separate species and lineages involved[6]. Others doubt that more than one lineage is present (though a separate lineage of 'robust australopithecines' is found after two and a half million years ago, for more than a million years).

Partly in order to keep things simple, but mainly because I think it reflects the true situation better, I will be using the term 'gracilins' for the whole pre-human sample. It is entirely to be expected that the earlier forms would be different from (and more chimp-like) than the later forms. Let us now look at the anatomy of this gracilin population. There are three main areas in which they depart from the chimpanzee lineage - posture and mode of walking, brain and braincase, and teeth and chewing apparatus.

Arguably the most important changes concern walking or locomotion. Chimps travel across the ground using their front extremities (hands) as well as feet for walking. Gracilin fossils clearly indicate individuals with a more upright posture, who walked on two legs, or bipedally. This is well indicated in later gracilin fossils, (of some two and a half to three and a half million years years old). Also there is a fine set of footprints from Laetoli, in Tanzania, of gracilins over three and a half million years old. These, and indications from yet earlier gracilins, are consistent with walking on two legs.

Both the 'feet' and the 'hands' of chimps can be used for holding or grasping things, but neither is as well suited for manipulation as human hands are. In gracilins the feet were slow to assume the form found in humans, which is specialised for walking; even later gracilins still have the big toe more widely splayed than humans. One of the most far-reaching results of bipedalism is that it frees the hands from walking, so that objects can be better manipulated, or more easily carried while travelling. The hand was also slow to assume its human form, but more complete hand fossils will be needed to document this process reliably. Chimps have long arms relative to their legs; comparison of the relative length of the fore-limbs and the hind-limbs places gracilins midway between chimps and modern humans.

The row of teeth in a chimpanzee has a dagger-like canine tooth which projects so far beyond the chewing surface that it is necessary to have a gap in the opposite toothrow to permit the jaws to close. Because the canines interlock, side-to-side chewing or grinding by the molars is precluded. Humans and gracilins have canine teeth of reduced size, and can thus grind or masticate sideways, as well as simply biting and crushing downwards.

Gracilins have large teeth. In a direct comparison, both the cheek teeth and the front teeth are larger than those of europeans (and most races). When we take into account that the gracilins were little more than half the weight of modern europeans, we can see that the disparity is very significant. The wear on gracilin teeth was also very marked, showing that they needed this large chewing surface. While ape toothrows are never 'crowded' together (because the essential gap in the row would close), both gracilin and human teeth tend to be crowded, and even misaligned as a result.

The size of the brain is indicated by the volume of the interior of the braincase, or cranium, in fossils. In chimps it is relatively small (around 350 to 400 cubic centimetres), and in the common ancestor it was probably no bigger. In gracilins the brain size seems to have been a little larger - at least in the later ones more in the order of 400 to 500 c.c.. Chimp and gorilla braincases are low and flattened. Gracilin braincases became more rounded or domed.

A more interesting comparison takes account of the body size or weight. Chimps, though short in stature are heavy (and strong). Gracilins, as their name suggests, are relatively light; perhaps they weighed, on average, about half as much as common chimps. Thus the ratios of brain weight to body weight are in the following order:-

chimp 1:130, gracilin 1:50, modern europeans 1:50. Clearly gracilins had moved close to humans on this measure[7].

Chimpanzees and other apes have a thick coat of fur or hair over almost the whole body, and the common ancestor almost certainly had the same. It is likely that gracilins retained the thick body hair cover, but all modern races have lost most of it. We shall examine in the next chapter why this happened.

We have considered the evidence from fossils of the gracilins at some length, because it provides the best avenue to forming a picture of their behaviour. Indeed it provides the only direct evidence for reconstructing this behaviour.

It is likely that the principle food elements eaten by chimpanzees (and by the last common ancestor of humans and chimps) would have continued to be important for the gracilin populations. These would include fruits, nuts, shoots and invertebrates. The question arises whether there was any significant shift in their diet or economy. The teeth remain very large relative to their body size, suggesting that it was still necessary to eat a larger bulk than humans now habitually do. (Also the absence of the dagger canines would remove the possibility of slicing open sugar cane or fruits with hard rinds, as gorillas do when feeding.)

Two changes may be suggested. The first is that eating of seeds from wild grasses played a more important part in the diet[8]. Chimpanzees, and probably the common ancestor, live or lived in rather dense tropical forest, where grasses and their seeds are rare. In the miocene, it is thought that the rainforest was much more extensive than now, but during the pliocene it contracted, and grassland expanded. Also the gracilins seem to have moved into the drier eastern side of Africa. All these factors would make a switch to eating more seeds likely. In addition the ability to grind food between the molars laterally, (in a way that is not possible for chimps and gorillas), would make it more feasible to get nutrition from such seeds. Seed picking would also provide a powerful boost to the selection for better thumb-finger co-ordination, because seeds are difficult to pick up with a chimpanzee-type hand.

The second possibility is an increase in 'scavenging' of meat from carnivore kills. We shall see in the next chapter that true human-type hunting is scarcely possible without stone tool flaking or similar technology. Further, the reduction of the canines in gracilins has made it less easy for them to kill or tear up small mammals than was the case with chimps, who were also much stronger. However scavenging from kills made by carnivores on the grassland plains, or in open wooded country, would now be much more feasible. Claims have been made in the case of at least one gracilin site (the Makapansgat 'limeworks' site in south Africa) that the bones accumulated in the level with the gracilin fossils were the parts which would be expected if scavenging had been practised. If this had been the case for the later gracilins, it would have been a kind of stepping stone to the regular hunting practised by humans proper. However the evidence suggests that the meat component of the diet of gracilins was still small; otherwise smaller teeth would presumably have sufficed.

The beginning of true technology is discussed in the next chapter. Here we need to note that no trace of the making of stone tools has been found in contexts earlier than about two and a half million years ago[1]. None of the gracilin fossils has apparently ever been found associated with contemporaneous stone tools. It seems sensible to adopt as a provisional conclusion that gracilins did not yet make such tools.

It has often been suggested in the past that wood or bone tools may have been made before stone tools. On closer inspection, this is not a satisfactory theory, because shaping wood and bone is only feasible with a sharp tool such as a stone flake. No one has ever suggested a plausible alternative technique available more than two and a half a million years ago. Even if grinding were feasible, no ground bone tools have been found, nor has any plausible use for them been suggested.

We therefore return to the question of toolusing which, as we have seen, is found in common chimps. Firstly it seems entirely plausible that unmodified or barely modified natural objects may have been used by the gracilins as tools, though for what purpose is not at present clear. As we have seen above, gracilins no longer used their hands in walking, and (probably as a result) these hands were able to evolve considerably in the direction of more efficient manipulation of 'instruments'. The short thumb, which chimps have, makes precision manipulation difficult, but we know that humans had an elongated thumb, opposable to the index finger, from an early time, and it is likely that later gracilins had already evolved in this direction. There was thus every opportunity for gracilins to manipulate better than chimps. Such objects as naturally sharp broken stones (which would sometimes be available) may well have been used in getting meat from carnivore kills.

The social organisation of gracilins can only be treated speculatively. Did they belong to loose communities like apes, with no family structure and no recognition of male or extended kinship? We shall see in the next chapter that there are good reasons for thinking that the marriage custom and the family came about as a result of males becoming 'professional' hunters, and bonding with wives, who concentrated on gathering and child rearing. In the absence of such a 'specialisation' by sex before true hunting appears, we must conclude that the chimp-style community would probably not have given way to the hunter-type family and band until true humans emerged.

There is some direct fossil evidence concerning the ability of gracilins to use speech. Two authorities have independently pointed out that on the insides of the skulls of very early humans, there are clear signs of the development of the two small areas in the brain which are known to be associated with speech[9]. These fossils date from around two million years ago. By contrast, the latest gracilins (of more than two and a half million years ago) seem, like the apes, to lack any clear sign of the emergence of these brain areas. The obvious conclusion is that speech was first developed in very early humans, and was not present in pre-humans.

However, bearing in mind that gracilins would not normally be carrying things in their mouths (unlike chimps who do this often), they may well have communicated using calls of some sort, on a much more regular basis than apes do. There is a strong possibility that, before true speech was developed, some form of high pitched vocalisation was practised by our distant ancestors. This would explain why humans have the higher register of voice used in singing, alongside that normally used in ordinary speech. In addition it would presumably have taken some time for natural selection to bring into being the speech areas, and the use of an advanced call system in the period around and before two and a half million years ago would explain why selection was operating to encourage the development of these brain areas at this time.

Call systems of higher primates, such as gibbons, are closed in the sense that the calls are not blended or run together. It has been suggested[10] that a vital step towards true language was the 'opening' of the call system by blending individual calls, in order to communicate more complicated ideas than could be transmitted with single noises. Possibly this process of opening was first achieved by the gracilins.

The thinking of chimpanzees seems, as noted in the preceding section, to be in some ways analogous to the most advanced pre-linguistic thinking in children, the advanced 'sensorimotor' stage of Piaget[see note 5]. We shall see in the next chapter that hunter-gatherers exhibit thought analogous to Piaget's next stage of development, which coincides usually with the first acquisition of speech. It seems unlikely that gracilins reached this; more likely they remained at the same broad level as chimps.

We move on in the next chapter to human history proper, with a study of the hunter-gatherer level of the first humans. The fossil evidence for human biological evolution will not be discussed here. It has only limited relevance to the remaining chapters, though it is of outstanding interest in itself, as well as being highly controversial.

Chapter THREE   THE LEVEL OF HUNTER-GATHERERS: Level I (the Paleoric)

We now consider the broad characteristics of level I, the hunter-gatherer level of cultural organisation.   This will be done in three main sections, and the prime emphasis will be on the contrasts with the preceding non-human level (the Bioric).

Section i **Technology, Economy and Demography**

Level I begins (according to our definition) with the first true toolmaking; this is also the definition most widely used by archaeologists, and other students of early man, for the beginning of humans (as opposed to pre-humans or apes). The earliest true toolmaking seems to have been stone tool making, and began as we noted in the previous chapter (see note 1) some two and a half million years ago. Recent researchers of chimpanzee behaviour have talked of "toolmaking" among common chimps. However true toolmaking or toolcraft[1], as practised even by early hunter-gatherers, was quite different from anything found among apes, as we will now try to make clear.

The first and most important criterion of human toolcraft is the use of a tool[2] in the process of **making** a tool or piece of equipment. In the case of stone toolmaking, which seems in the beginning to have been the key to the development of all other technology, a hammerstone or striker was the usual tool used in flaking rocks like flint or quartzite.

The second criterion of toolcraft is the making or crafting of tools to a set and regular pattern. This is the very essence of true (i.e. human) culture[3]. The third criterion is anticipation. It is normal for tools to be made before the immediate need for them has arisen. Ready made tools are regularly carried, when it is anticipated that they may be needed.

If we glance for a moment at what is known of chimpanzee tool behaviour, we find that using a tool to make a tool is not normal; as far as I know, it has never been found in wild chimpanzees. Shaping tools to a set and regular, or culturally imposed, pattern is unknown in chimps, or any other (non-human) animals. There does not seem to be any evidence for tools made in anticipation or carried on the daily round, by chimps or any other animals.

The fact that chimps have been shown to practise rather advanced toolusing, and **not** toolcraft, makes them and the research on them **more** interesting, and not less important. This is because, as a result, chimp's tool behaviour can be seen a a kind of prototype or stepping stone to the first toolcraft, which is much more valuable for our understanding of the evolution of culture, than if they had already possessed unquestionable toolmaking. We may also reiterate the point made in the last chapter that the notion of true toolmaking in wood or bone **before** the beginning of stone tool flaking is not supported by the evidence, and would make no sense from a practical point of view.

A second distinctive characteristic of all known level I peoples is hunting; this is why the vernacular term hunter-gatherers is in essence appropriate for this level[4]. Once again unfortunately, the distinction between early humans and chimpanzees has (as in the case of toolcraft) been confused, by loose usage of the term hunting. Chimps are known to kill animals, and do sometimes eat them. To clarify this matter is even more important in this case, than it was with toolmaking. In fact the 'huntcraft' of early humans has many more distinct criteria than was the case with toolcraft.

In known hunter-gatherers, hunting is a regular and substantial contributor to the diet, especially as the source of protein so important for human nutrition. The hunter sets out regularly with the specific intention of hunting. The hunter searches purposefully for prey, long before it is visible, because he already has a notion of what animals are likely to be found and where. He is a 'professional' in the sense that he gains his livelihood by hunting, and thinks of himself as a hunter. Hunt weapons and tools are fundamental to the craft of hunting, and especially to skinning and butchering the animals taken. Kills, or meat taken from them, are brought back to the camp, whenever this is practicable. Alternatively the camp is moved to the kill site if transporting is too difficult. The animals are carefully butchered; and then the meat is shared among the family or band (according to rules based on kinship); the females regularly get a fair share.

By contrast, chimpanzees exhibit none of these features of huntcraft. For them, 'hunting' is an irregular and rather rare activity. Its contribution to the diet is small (see chapter II, note 2), and for females and their young it is smaller than for the males. Chimpanzees do not apparently set out regularly, if ever, with the specific intention of hunting. It seems that chimps spot their prey by chance, and then pursue it in a rather frenzied way: At other times they seem happy to live peacably close to the same animal species, and even play with them. Advance planning of hunts seems to be unknown. Certainly there is no indication that they see hunting as a living.

Hunt weapons and tools are not used by chimps; they have instead long dagger-like canine teeth, strong claw-like finger nails and enormous muscular strength. They have little problem tearing prey apart, and this seems to be their normal killing technique. Chimp kills are not brought back to the 'camp'. Nor are they carefully butchered or skinned. The males responsible for each kill expect to eat most, or all, of the meat. Females and juveniles may beg for a little meat, but they have no customary right. There are some other differences, but it should be obvious that the occasional kill is a quite different kind of thing from the huntcraft practised by humans of level I.

We may add here that the practicalities of the hunter-gatherer way of life mean that settled or sedentary living all the year round is not feasible, and such level I societies are largely nomadic. As we define level I here, any society which achieves sedentism, or even something close to sedentism[5], has stepped beyond the bounds of level I (into the interlevel which follows it, or to the next level).

A third major feature, which represents a distinct advance for humans over their pre-human ancestors, is routine meateating. Although there are other reasons for 'hunting' - eradicating predators or as sport, for example - there is little doubt that it was for the meat, and not for any other principle reason, that hunting was practised in level I.

The hunter-gatherer diet is, as the name suggests, a combination of two major components. One is gathered mainly by females, and the second (principally flesh) component involves a variety of techniques practised by men. The 'female' segment includes much vegetable food, but also insects, grubs, molluscs and small animals of many kinds. The 'male' component involves more traversing and running, which would be impracticable for females with young. Sometimes fish are important, sometimes reptiles or amphibians, and sometimes it was birds. But in general, across the whole sample which we know, mammals are the commonest prey. Sometimes these are quite small, but increasingly in level I, hunters are quite capable of taking even the largest animals – elephants, rhinos and giraffes. However carnivores are rarely taken, because they are not a good source of meat. The hunter, out on his trek, will regularly gather and eat small quantities of plant food or invertebrates, as he goes.

The relative proportion of the two components varies greatly. In the equatorial latitudes, vegetable food makes up well over half the bulk of the food, but rarely more than 75 to 80%. It must be remembered that meat is a high energy food, which provides much greater tissue replacement and nutrition in general; more especially meat provides much more protein per unit of weight or bulk. It is also a provider of valuable vitamin B^{12}, rare or absent in non-flesh foods. Hunter-gatherers tend to have much less of a problem with vitamin or mineral deficiencies than did later farming peoples.

In the polar latitudes, meat from mammals and fish constitutes the great majority of all food. The vegetable component can be as small as zero, though the stomach contents of kills may well contain, and thus provide, some partly digested plant food. Between the polar and tropical latitudes, there is a general gradation from the dominant meat diet to the dominant vegetable diet. During the ice ages, the meat dominant sector would have extended further towards the equator.

Although, in the past, the 'macho' aspect of the hunting era has occasionally been overstated, recent sneering at a "man the mighty hunter" syndrome is misplaced and tendentious. Male hunting **was** the key to the hunter-gatherer way of life, even though hunters were often quite gentle or relaxed about their task.

Neither apes nor any non-humans wear or wore clothes. All known hunter-gatherers seem to wear some clothing, though this can be minimal in warm latitudes or extensive and sophisticated in cold latitudes. (It is true that the Fuegians of southernmost South America are supposed to have hunted naked sometimes in freezing conditions, but they also wore more extensive fur clothing on other occasions.) There seems to be a near universal inclination to cover the genital regions with some kind of 'loin cloth'. The prime purpose here seems not to be for warmth or protection, but a 'social' purpose of some kind, presumably observing an unspoken taboo on exposing the genitalia or any signals of arousal they may give.

All known human societies use some sort of artificial shelter as part of their culture. By contrast apes, and other mammals, construct no artificial shelters. The most that chimpanzees do is to 'arrange' a kind of bed or nest. It takes no more than a few minutes to bend down branches or fronds, until they make a comfortable night nest. Often they are not re-used a second night. A single chimp (or a mother with baby) occupies each nest.

Hunter-gatherers (including all those known ethnographically, and a number of cases from the archaeological record) regularly construct shelters, and occupy them for the (usually short) duration of their stay. Sometimes they are like wind breaks, others are more like tents. Unlike the chimpanzee 'nests', they regularly shelter a family unit of some kind. Hunters often sleep huddled together for warmth, and will use a bed covering, if they need it. The elaborateness of the housing arrangements will depend mainly on how inhospitable the climate is.

Apes use their hands for moving around. Chimps normally walk on all fours, resting a lot of weight on their knuckles. Also chimps and some other apes climb and swing through trees. Either way their hands are not free to carry things, though they may use their mouths. Already our pre-human ancestors (the gracilins) had developed upright walking, and had their hands more often free.

Hunter-gatherers walk or run on two legs, with a well balanced upright posture. Their hands are thus free to carry things, and they also sling bags or containers over their shoulders. This is the beginning of transport proper. Usually they avoid transporting heavy or bulky objects. Game kills or the meat from them are sometimes carried to the camp; but the camp is moved to the kill if it is distant or heavy. Light objects, such as knives or spears or bows and arrows are carried. Women almost always carry some kind of digging stick. Dwellings are rarely carried, though some small tents may be portable[6].

Apes move round their territory while foraging, but rarely travel far. Among hunter-gatherers, longer treks are more typical. Hunters are known to pursue game by running doggedly after it. The game is normally much faster over short distances, but soon has to rest to avoid heat exhaustion. Cases are recorded of hunters pursuing game for hours or days, and they often eventually get their prey. (This is presumably the origin of the human capacity for marathon running.) Humans seem to be able to avoid heat exhaustion, because they have adapted to dissipate their heat. Unlike apes, they have little visible body hair and more numerous sweat glands. The loss of thick body hair or fur is probably an adaptation to just this problem, and accordingly would probably date from the early days of hunting.

Great apes are very strong, (regularly more so than humans). They use only muscle power. Hunter-gatherers rely mainly on muscle power, but certainly in the later stages, this is augmented by simple devices. The spear thrower was used both by ethnographically known hunters, like the australian aborigines, and by archaeologically known hunters of the late ice age in Europe. Its use is the equivalent of having a much longer arm for throwing; it increases leverage and throwing distance. The simple hunting bow harnesses inertia, and can send a projectile much further and harder than the unaided arm. Bows were also employed to rotate spindles, as in the case of the bow drill, used for making holes or for making fire. These techniques were still simple, but they represented a significant advance over the pre-human level.

Neither the concept of trade nor of giving is applicable to the ape level. Hunter-gatherers by contrast do indulge in sharing and 'gift giving' as a social rather than an economic activity. Sometimes gift giving was entirely symbolic, as in the exchange of bows, which were more or less identical. Trade was rare between hunting groups; but some examples of the exchange of objects are known[7]. Nothing that can sensibly be called wealth existed among hunter-gatherers. Their economy was of the subsistence type. Nomadism did not allow surpluses to be accumulated[8].

Biological consequences of human culture: demography, health and ecology

We will begin with population density. The foraging way of life which preceded agriculture will not support a high density of population over large areas. Thus the population of both apes and hunter-gatherers is low by comparison with that of tribal farmers, who replaced them in many areas; the latter were regularly able to sustain a density of about one hundred times greater than hunter-gatherers[9], as we shall see in the next chapter.

The big difference between apes and hunter-gatherers is not in density, but in the total area occupied. The apes, in common with most other primate species, occupied relatively small areas (less than a million sq. kms. for the bonobo chimp, about one and a half million for the gorilla, and probably less than three million for the common chimps). Early humans spread over not just Africa, but much of Eurasia, occupying (even in the first sub-level of level I) up to sixty million sq. kms; and this continued to expand. Hunter-gatherers evidently enjoyed a much greater adaptability, of which technology was clearly a significant part.

We shall see that changes in the average percentage of death before maturity (in these figures meaning under sixteen years old) are extremely obvious when one compares hunter-gatherers with the industrial era. The figures for earlier levels are necessarily scanty and imprecise, but they all point to the same conclusion, namely that premature mortality is high in the earliest levels (apes and hunter-gatherers) and decreases steadily as one passes through the five levels, but most obviously during the industrial era[10]. For both the ape and pre-human level and for the hunter-gatherer level, the percentage of premature mortality is over half – probably over sixty percent for the earliest humans and for apes, and perhaps in the order of fifty to sixty percent for later hunter-gatherers[10].

The figures for the average expectancy of life are slightly more reliable. They tell the same story, but here, as one would expect, average age at death increases over the previous level, rather than decreases; and again the increase is greatest in the industrial level (V)[10]. In the earlier levels, when infant and child mortality is very high, we get a much higher result if we calculate expectation of life only from those who survived to fifteen, rather than at birth, (but for the late twentieth century industrial level, the two are much the same).

The scanty indications for the ape and pre-human level suggest an average life expectancy at birth of about ten years, and for those lucky enough to survive to fifteen an average somewhere in the order of eighteen to twenty-three years, perhaps averaging close to twenty years. For the hunter-gatherer level, indications suggest an average 'birth' expectancy of perhaps about fifteen years; while the average for those who attain fifteen years is perhaps in the range twenty four to thirty years, increasing among the later hunter-gatherers to as much as twenty five to thirty two years. Male life expectancy seems on available evidence to have been higher on average than female expectancy. (For the industrial era, as we shall see, female expectancy is higher than for males, and both sexes by the latest part of this level can expect over seventy years, even at birth.[10])

Health. In the pre-human level, as represented for example by living apes, there is nothing approaching medical care. They rely on innate responses to ill health, which may occasionally lead them to take internal or external treatments of some value[11]. Hunter-gatherers, who possess a store of culture passed on from generation to generation by language, have elementary notions of medical care. (Even the tasmanian aborigines, who seem to represent the most primitive stratum of human culture which has survived to modern times, are reported to have used 'herbs', and to have cut or manipulated the body in an attempt to heal sickness.)

All known hunter-gatherers in our sample have a person, usually called a shaman, who is credited with the ability to deal with sickness. (These shamans are, as we shall see below, primarily 'religious' figures or 'magicians', who are thought to be able to 'deal with' spirits.) The very existence of such a figure, even if the resulting cure rate was poor, represents a step beyond the animal level.

Alteration of the environment.

Apes make no more alteration to their environment than most animals. Indeed elephants and hippos can make a lot more impact, and create sizeable clearings in woodland. Probably early humans caused little more modification of their environment than apes, and their pursuit and killing of prey would make neither more nor less impact than a typical carnivore.

Later hunter-gatherers did develop some practices which are without parallel in the animal world, and in so doing did cause some lasting change to the environment. The best example is the 'firing' of the landscape. This intentional burning of the vegetation is not feasible in plantless terrain, nor in wet tropical rainforest, but in environments like open woodland or scrubby bush or in grassland with or without scattered trees or shrubs, it is feasible, provided that the hunters had the ability to make or obtain fire. It is known to have been practised by the australian aborigines, and by the post-glacial 'mesolithic' hunters of Europe. Apparently it not only improves the quantity of new growth, but also the quality. This encourages more game, and thus in due course hunters can enjoy an increase in the available food supply. (Something similar is practised by national park conservationists in Britain, where it is called 'swaling'; usually it is done every seven years.)

In two regions that were first occupied late on in human evolution, major extinctions of larger mammals occurred. This was probably due to human interference, either direct or indirect, because it happened in each case shortly after hunter-gatherers arrived. In Australia and New Guinea this dates from about fifty thousand years ago, and in the Americas nearer twelve thousand years ago. These have been called 'overkills'. Nothing on this scale has been noted from Eurasia and Africa, where humans had enjoyed a considerably longer 'apprenticeship'.

Section ii **Social, Political and Military**

Several features of the social organisation of hunter-gatherers are clearly distinct from those of the preceding level of apes and the pre-human gracilins. Perhaps the most fundamental is the pairing or bond between the male hunter and the female gatherer. Part of the explanation for this 'marriage' is economic. The male hunter can usually capture enough game for himself and his 'family', and the female can gather enough for herself and her 'family'.

The second point is that human juveniles mature more slowly than do apes or most non-humans, and they have to be fed and protected for considerably more years.[12]

Although this biological trend is variable in different groups, and was probably not as marked in earlier humans, there is reason to think that it had already begun at the time of the earliest toolmakers. The male hunter cannot contribute as much to this prolonged care of children, because he is not able to suckle his babies, and he cannot take them with him on a strenuous and taxing hunt. The female gatherer on the other hand is well adapted to the task of coping with most of the child rearing while her husband is away hunting. These two factors make a marriage arrangement highly 'desirable' for both partners, who of course can only pass on their genes by having viable surviving children. (That they would not themselves have thought in these terms, does not in any way alter the fact such behaviour would be selected for, just like physical characteristics.)

Because the male can procure enough game for a wife and some children, but normally could not regularly produce enough to feed two or more wives and their offspring, the marriage is usually monogamous. However marriage to several wives (known as polygyny) is occasionally found in hunter-gatherers, but more than two at a time is very rare. Such polygyny is more likely to occur in tropical or warm latitudes, where gathered food tends to be much more plentiful than game. At the opposite extreme, in the arctic, where gathered food is rare or negligible, we sometimes encounter 'wife-sharing'. Females may be rarer than males if female infanticide is practised, and this can lead to polyandry (a woman with several husbands). The important point is that monogamy is by far the most normal situation.

The male-female pairing in humans is more than a convenient symbiotic arrangement. One of the most distinctive features of human culture, as opposed to non-human behaviour, is that there are ceremonies or rites for important occasions, and this is the case for marriage, as with the other 'life-crisis rites' (birth, puberty and death). However simple this marriage rite is, it will follow the 'custom' of the people in question, and those who live in the area will know of the marriage and respect it.

The existence of a marriage custom, along with the normal outcome of one or more babies, automatically creates what we call a family. The family is the basic 'building block' on which is erected a system of kinship. All known hunter-gatherers have or had kinship arrangements, and kinship is more important to people at this level than it is to people at the highest levels. Kinship in primitive peoples usually extends further than in modern western societies. The family already involves the idea of generations (children, parents, grandparents). Then there is the idea of collaterals (siblings, cousins etc.), and marriage introduces the idea of 'in-laws' or affines. Kinship also suggests the idea of ancestors. (Non-literate peoples find it hard to deal with persons who are not 'relatives', and so there is sometimes a flourishing business of creating fictitious relationships, so that everyone is put at ease. Total strangers and researchers from across the globe have been incorporated in this way.)

Closely bound up with kinship is the idea of incest; hunter-gatherers and tribal farmers often exclude a much wider range of people as permissible marriage or sex partners than modern westerners do. A taboo on incest is virtually universal among peoples of these two levels, but their stories often contain references to or hints of incest. They seem to have a kind of love-hate feeling for incest, and view it with fascination yet horror.

The family is fundamental and advantageous in level I. The family also provides the context in which elementary teaching may take place. This is mainly done by example, but partly by verbal instruction. Lastly food sharing, as mentioned in the preceding section, is absolutely routine in the family. It is universally expected and effectively obligatory.

It is now time to contrast hunter-gatherers with apes and other pre-human populations. The differences are quite clear. Neither chimpanzees nor gorillas have an enduring male-female pairing, formalised by any kind of ceremony. The family unit, of a male, a female and their children, does not exist. The cultural division of labour, even by sex, is effectively non-existent. (Females suckle and nurse, while males do not, but this is biological not cultural.) The routine food sharing found universally in the hunter-gatherer family is quite absent in non humans. The most that is found among apes is 'tolerated scrounging'. It is difficult to avoid incest consciously in ape populations, because the young rarely or never know who their father is.

There are further social features that contrast hunter-gatherers with the non-human or pre-human level. Several families normally live together in what anthropologists usually call a band. Ethnographic observations of surviving hunting peoples reveal that the size of this band is regularly of the order of twenty five to thirty individuals. If it grows much larger than this, it often splits into more than one band. The families in the band are almost invariably related by known ties of kinship. For example the men are often related in the male line, or as an alternative the women may be related in the female line. A common situation is one where the males stay in the band they were born into, and their sisters marry out of the band into a neighbouring band[13]. This 'band exogamy' has the effect of avoiding incest, and establishing friendly relations with neighbouring bands.

A group of bands invariably belongs to a much larger unit or grouping, which always has a name. The people of each band talk of themselves as belonging 'ethnically' to this larger grouping, which has a distinct language or dialect. It has been referred to as a tribe, but this term is more appropriately used for a rather different kind of grouping found in tribal farmers, so we shall use the term paleo-tribe. There are usually something like twenty hunter bands in this larger grouping. Typically it numbers around five hundred people, (because twenty bands of twenty five people makes up such a number,) but it can be larger or smaller. If the community in apes is broadly analogous to the hunter band, they certainly have no equivalent of the paleo-tribe.

Now we move to a further, rather surprising, feature of hunter-gatherer society. Its people are egalitarian, in the sense that they do not recognise any formal status or formal leadership. Actually their notion of egalitarianism goes further than this, as we shall see in the next section. At the same time it is only a <u>form</u> of egalitarianism, because individuals know perfectly well that some people are stronger or more skilled or more intelligent than others.

In each band there is usually a 'headman', but his position is entirely informal. He has no real power, and he cannot order people to do his bidding, because nobody would take any notice. He holds his 'role' as a result of a general consensus that he is the best choice. If there is a problem, he may discuss it with the 'elder' members of the band, acting as a kind of chairman. If general agreement is reached, this will be acted upon. If disagreement or the personality clash is too strong, the band may split. Egalitarianism does not prevent a tradition of respect for the elders, (who with a life expectancy of under thirty years are not usually going to be very old).

By contrast the larger 'paleo-tribe' does not have a headman or leader, and rarely or never acts in unison. The leader would have to be 'separated' in some way from his band, and this is not usually practicable. As we shall see in the next chapter, the 'true' tribe, found in farming peoples, usually does have a leader, whose leadership transcends that of the small villages and other groups within it. There is thus some political cohesion in a true tribe, but there is no formal cohesion in a hunter-gatherer paleo-tribe.

A further function of the paleo-tribe is in connection with marriage. If it is customary for girls (or alternatively boys) to marry and reside outside the band, they will tend to finish up in neighbouring bands of the same paleo-tribe. This will be preferable to going to a different paleo-tribe, because that will have a different language or dialect, and a girl or boy will prefer a partner who they can easily understand. The paleo-tribe can thus act as a kind of marriage bureau.

All these social features contrast with the situation in the preceding level. Chimps have a hierarchy, and are not egalitarian. The hunter-gatherer headman is quite unlike the dominant or 'alpha' male in chimps. There is of course no language or dialect tribe in apes.

We may now turn to the subject of hostilities. In accordance with the spirit (or rather zeitgeist) of the last thirty years, it has often been implied that hunter-gatherers and chimpanzees are markedly non-violent and peacable. Like many fashionable contemporary views, this one has no foundation in fact. There is ample evidence that apes and hunter-gatherers regularly indulged in violence, killing, and even small scale extermination[14]. Fighting or killing among hunter-gatherers is distinct from that found among apes, mainly to the extent that it involves the use of weapons like spears and clubs. These are basically the same 'tools' that were made and used for killing game.

As we shall see in the next section, all death, illness and misfortune was often conceived by hunter-gatherers as the result of 'malign' magic. An 'inquest' tends to find someone responsible for this. Following a killing, it is common for a revenge party, from the close kin of the victim, to try to avenge the deed in some way. That the 'theoretical' principle of automatic killing in revenge does not always take place is evident, because otherwise the population would quickly be reduced to single figures.

Section iii **Communication, Thought and Religion**

Hunter-gatherers have speech and language of very much the same kind as all human societies now have. As we noted in the preceding chapter, evidence from the interior of the braincase suggests that both the main speech areas were already developed in humans of about two million years ago, whereas skulls of their predecessors (the later gracilins) do not seem to show development of these areas. The simplest and most obvious conclusion to draw from this is that speech developed more or less at the time of the first appearance of humans and of their culture. Apes lack the development of the speech areas, and modification of the vocal tract to allow speech, and thus it is no surprise that in the wild they are not capable of speech[15]. The acquisition of speech is of outstanding long-term importance (comparable to the development of technology). What function speech fulfils when it first appears is not entirely clear. The view that it promotes social interaction and co-operation is perhaps the most satisfactory answer yet[16]. It may be that co-operation was vital in the earliest hunting.

A second ability which follows closely from speech is that of myth making. All known hunter-gatherer societies construct, remember and pass on myths[17]. Myths may be defined as sacred stories, (but I would agree with those who would restrict the term to those stories 'by which a society lives'). Underlying myth making is a particular kind of thought – mythic thought. In level I, mythic thought does not employ logic or consistency. Internal contradictions are routinely accepted with no qualms. Reasons are not offered. There is no notion of cause and effect, (only of 'will'). Everything is personalised, so that objectivity plays no part. There is little interest in clearly differentiating or distinguishing separate phenomena. Incommens-urateness is routinely allowed. (In one australian aboriginal myth, a man is struck, and blood gushes out. Then the valley fills with blood - and soon everyone in the valley is drowned!). All this kind of thinking may be called 'prae-logical'.

It is possible to see four vague principles underlying all mythic thought of the hunter-gatherer level. We have already encountered one in the preceding section – the social (or socio-mythic) principle of 'egalitarianism'. This principle does not just hold that humans are undifferentiated by status or hierarchy. This egalitarianism includes the physical world (rocks, fire, stars, clouds etc), and extends through the entire biological sphere (plants and animals as well as humans), and includes the revered mythic ancestors who appear in the stories. The egalitarian principle effectively rules out any possibility of 'gods'.

The three remaining principles are more obviously 'spiritual' or sacred in character. To the mind of the hunter-gatherers, everything they encounter (be it rock, tree or animal) consists of two 'elements' – the body or substance on the one hand, and the 'spirit' on the other. The spirit (for want of a better word) is seen as vaguely analogous to breath, wind, mind or will; obviously it cannot (normally) be seen. The body is simply the 'shell' in which the real person or will exists. The spirit com-ponent is the owner or animator of the body, and is evidently the more important component. Spirits can of course move around as they wish, or from body to body, and often more than one type of spirit is seen as operating in a body.

The origins of this concept are not difficult to find. For all their limited experience, hunter-gatherers are aware of dreams or trances. (Indeed 'altered states of consciousness' seem to be commoner for them than is normal in western society.) And they are aware of 'expiration' at death. The 'death rattle' of breath (which departs as people die) is to them 'obviously' the departure of an invisible part of the deceased, who then breathes no more. Dreamers regularly find themselves 'visiting' other places, but on waking discover that their body has not moved, as confirmed by their companions in the camp. Trances similarly involve an apparent departure of the real person from their body. The simplest explanation of these observations would be to accept that the real person is a spirit. (Anthropologists often call such a concept of active spirits animism.)

Since the hunter-gatherer form of animism extends across every thing (from rocks to the ancestors), I have characterised it as 'pan-animism'[18]. Once this principle is understood, it goes a long way to explaining the 'egalitarianism' described above; if everything has a spirit of much the same kind, and especially if the spirit moves from tree to rock to person, this naturally puts all phenomena on a more or less equal footing.

The next 'spiritual' principle also has a reasonably obvious connection with pan-animism. If the spirit is the driving force in any phenomenon, and we need to change it in some way, because it is being harmful or inconvenient, then it is the spirit we must address. In all hunter-gatherer societies there are people who are thought to have some special skill or ability to contact and deal with spirits. The most widely used name for these is the shaman[19]. Shamanesses are also found, but are rarer.

Shamans use a variety of techniques, but these almost always include trickery or conjuring of some kind. There is a widespread idea that the shaman can go on a 'journey' to persuade spirits to co-operate in some way; a favourite is a journey to the moon. In these journeys, and in other performances, the shaman often needs to fall into a trance. All sorts of avenues to altered states of consciousness are used to achieve this. Sometimes hallucinogens, such as mushrooms or tobacco, are employed, but there are many other techniques, like self hypnosis or violent dance with head shaking. The shaman goes into a trance or sleep during a 'consultation'. He is then thought to go on his journey, and those consulting him wait with his 'body'. On his 'return', he recounts the journey, usually described as a success . The people assume he was away, and regard his body as an unimportant shell to which he returns. In addition shamans are widely credited with the ability to perform 'transformations' of themselves or others. Thus we see that, in a sense, shamanic magic is little more than applied animism.

The last principle is simultaneously the simplest and the most complex. Basically it is little more than a pervasive sense of reverence for, and linkage with, the whole mysterious world. It was always vague and rested partly on a prae-logical failure to distinguish the separate phenomena in their confusing world. The hunter-gatherer feels a sacred or spiritual bond with the whole known world. The idea is rooted in the myths concerning the ancestors, and the time of 'origins' or events which are thought to have brought their world into being. The people yearn to be re-united with these ancestors and events, not in the past, still less in the future (neither of which concepts exists clearly at this level), but in a kind of 'eternal present'.

Here is where the complexities start. The principal 'symbol' of this bond is (or was) the combination or 'confusion' of people with animals (or sometimes other phenomena). The english word which comes nearest to this idea of composite nature is 'therianthropy' (an amalgamation of man and beast). The ancestors are regularly therianthropic. This dual nature can take many forms. The characters may be part human and part animal, or they may be conceived as changing readily between two or more forms. The idea of transformation is very typical of hunter-gatherer thought, and is particularly associated with shamanic activity.

Totemism is probably the best known form of therianthropy. This occurs when an individual or group 'adopts' an animal (or other phenomenon, like the moon) as a kind of 'brother' or alter ego. The thing adopted is the totem, and the person who adopts it is a totemite. Therianthropy (along with pan-animism and shamanic magic) does genuinely seem to be a universal of the hunter-gatherer level. But totemism, in its strict sense, is found only in some level I societies. Nevertheless it remains a significant and distinctive phenomenon.

In the absence of a suitable existing term, I have referred to this last principle of mythic thought as the 'pan-cosmic sacred bond'. Individual hunter-gatherer peoples do have terms which seem to refer to this principle. For example the Aranda 'tribe' of australian aborigines use the term 'alcheringa', (often translated into english as 'dreaming' or 'dreamtime'). But we need to realise that such terms often cover several meanings, which modern thought would try to separate. Alcheringa can refer to the 'ancestor-time', and also to the idea of transformation or metamorphosis, as well as being a normal term for dreams.

Among the Inuit (or eskimo) the term 'sila' is used, apparently in part at least, for the concept of such a sacred 'bond'. In Africa we find the term 'ntum' among the San (or bushmen), and 'megbe' among the congo pygmies; these words also seem to include the idea of a universal sacred bond. As it happens, the latin word 'religio', literally a kind of 'link back' (to an unspecified or vague world or past), can also be seen as originally a term for the 'sacred bond'. Indeed this might be the best single word to use, because it seems that all later religion is to some extent derived from this primal 'religio' of the hunter-gatherer level.[20].

Myth seems to be universal in ethnographically known hunter-gatherer societies. What is perhaps even more surprising is that all thought at this level is imbued with mythic ideas, if not pure myth. To put it another way, there is no secular segment in the 'world' of hunter-gatherers.

Does human type thinking necessarily involve language? Psychologists have long known that an individual human can develop human thought, even in cases where because of deafness or dumbness, normal speech is not possible for them[21]. At the same time there is experimental evidence that coaching in language can help the mental development of a backward child. Evidently individuals in normal language-using groups can develop thought, even if speech is impossible for them; but it seems likely that if a whole society lacked language, human type thought could not develop in it. The acquisition of language by early hunter-gatherers must have given an enormous boost to the development of thought, as it does in young children today. Thought and language probably evolved together.

When I first began serious research into the thought of humans at the earlier levels of culture, it never crossed my mind that the process and sequence of the development of thought, as it occurs in modern western children, might be the key to understanding the evolution of thought in the earlier levels of human society, but surprisingly this turned out to be the case.

A number of previous researchers have argued that the stages in the development of children's thought, first seriously studied by the swiss cognitive psychologist Jean Piaget, could be helpful in the quest to understand earlier stages of human thought[22]. In one of the most perceptive books on the behaviour of apes and other primates,

Alison Jolly pointed out that Piaget's scheme is useful in studying primate 'thought'; lower primates for example have a 'trial and error' form of thought (Piaget's sub-stage 5 of the first stage – sensorimotor), and ape thought is to some extent analogous to the final sub-stage of this first ('infant') stage[23].

In a very erudite study of primitive thought as found in non-literate peoples, known from ethnography, Christopher Hallpike argues that these peoples in their collective thought did not move beyond Piaget's second main stage[23]. Modifications of, and corrections to, Piaget's scheme in recent decades have actually made it fit the levels of human culture better than had originally seemed the case.

It turns out to be the first of the two sub-stages making up Piaget's second main stage in the development of thought[24] which has clear analogies with the 'mythic' thought of hunter-gatherers. It is called the pre-conceptual sub-stage. Piaget lists a series of characteristics of this sub-stage. Firstly pre-conceptual thought exhibits a complete absence of logic; indeed reasons are never given. We have already seen above that this is a characteristic of the mythic thought of hunter-gatherers.

Secondly pre-conceptual thinking is described by Piaget as highly 'centrated'. This basically means a sort of 'one-track' mind, incapable of coping with more than one variable. (For example if a child is asked to divide a collection of apples into those that are big and red and those that are small and green, it fails. Either all the red ones are put together or all the big ones.) This inability to follow two strands of thought simultaneously, obviously explains the routine acceptance of contradiction in the myths.

Thirdly, play in this sub-stage regularly involves **pretence** rather any attempt to imitate reality. This is rather similar to the creation and ritual enactment of mythical stories. Fourthly pre-conceptual notions do not refer to individuals with a stable identity, in different times and places. This is very much like the stories in which 'characters' repeatedly transform into new shapes or creatures. It is also in accord with the observation that different versions of the same stories portraying characters in varying forms seem to leave hunter-gatherers quite unfazed; all versions seem to be equally acceptable to them.

Fifthly pre-conceptual thought exhibits a tendency to link various objects and events together, although there are no reasonable grounds for doing so; (Piaget called this syncretism). We have already seen examples of this kind of thing among hunter-gatherers. Therianthropy and totemism link people to animals or things for no discernible reason, and again the entire 'sacred bond' links together everything, however diverse, or even harmful, on what appear to be purely emotional grounds.

Finally Piaget discussed at length three features of pre-conceptual thought which he called participation, magic and animism[24]. Participation was defined as the relation between two beings or phenomena, regarded as partially identical, or as having a direct influence on one another, although there is no spatial contact nor intelligible causal connection; (perhaps this should be seen as essentially the same as the fifth characteristic, mentioned above). Obviously this has a lot in common with the links we find in mythic thought, such as therianthropy and the sacred bond.

For Piaget, 'magic' was simply the use children (or people) thought they could make of participation (as defined above) to alter reality. This is of course almost exactly the same, in different words, as the principle of shamanic magic discussed earlier.

Lastly it was stated by Piaget that 'animism' was particularly typical of the pre-conceptual mode of thought. He defined it as the practice of endowing things with life and consciousness, adding that it was to be expected that a young child will regard inert objects as living and conscious. It is quite evident that Piaget's 'animism' is in effect identical with what we have already noted as the typical hunter-gatherer view of pan-animism - that *everything* is alive and spirit-bearing.

A similar characterisation of the thought of primitive humans as compared to apes and other higher animals was made by a contemporary of Piaget, Henri Frankfort (and his colleagues at the Oriental Institute of Chicago) in the1940s[25]. He said that the animal mode of thought consisted of 'passive', emotional and unarticulated understanding or impressions. Whereas the primitive human mode of thought was personalised, being of an *I-and-thou* form. As we shall see in chapter 5, this 'personalised' mode of thought survived, according to Frankfort, as the dominant form into the time of archaic states. Frankfort's interpretation is compatible with, and very similar to, the one which emerges from incorporating Piaget's scheme.

Hopefully the examples given above suffice to indicate that hunter-gatherer thought has much more in common with Piaget's pre-conceptual sub-stage than would be expected if they were not in some way part of the same phenomenon. Obviously further investigation of this link is needed, but enough has been established to justify using the pre-conceptual sub-stage as a working model of the thought of level I societies.

We may conclude our investigation of thought, communication and religion in the earliest levels, by emphasising the ways in which level I contrasts with the pre-human level. Apes and pre-humans, having no speech, possessed only mental images or symbols. By contrast level I people were able to employ verbal 'symbols' as well, and later hunter-gatherers also added pictorial symbols to the repertoire (notably the well known cave art). Pre-humans had no myth or religion of any kind. Ritual (in any strict sense) was not practised at this level, nor were two features – dance and chant – which seem likely to have originated in ritual. In contrast hunter-gatherers practised these things over a long period.

Apes have none of the features of mythic thought, which are reflected in Piaget's second stage of thought, but as we have seen hunter-gatherers did have this kind of thought. Apes do not practise burial or any kind of corpse ritual. Indeed it is hard to justify use of the words custom or culture for any of their behaviour, if this means any more than behaviour with some learning involved. Customs are evident in known hunter-gatherers, and some form of burial or corpse ritual is found, (at least in the two latest sub-levels).

No doubt these differences are partly related to the fact that pre-humans and apes had smaller brains than humans. Only in the largest apes did the brain size exceed 500 c.c.. During the hunter-gatherer period, the brain size quite soon reached 1000 c.c.. Peoples in Europe and western Asia in the later pleistocene (from about a quarter of a million years ago onwards) had brain sizes in the order of 1500 c.c.

There is an 'extra' sector of human behaviour, which the western mind is inclined to separate sharply from the three already considered. It concerns 'leisure', 'games' and 'aesthetics' or arts. In level V, this is for many people the most important sector, while in levels I and 0, it hardly exists at all; but it needs to be briefly examined.

Although hunter-gatherers have long periods of 'leisure', when they are not engaged on some necessary activity, it is not a category that they would recognise, nor are there any particular organised 'leisure' activities. Their whole world – 'leisure' and 'work' - is intimately bound up with their 'religion'. The ceremonies or rites associated with their religion (for example the 'dreaming' of the australian aborigines) were the highest pleasure and contentment they knew.

Just as young apes or domestic animals play, so all juvenile humans do. In each case their play tends to develop skills which will be useful later on in life. Play in hunter-gatherers will encourage skills of manipulation, or use of weapons like spears or boomerangs; by contrast apes' play would not involve any weapons skills. Similarly play in later levels tends to reflect those levels; and in late level V, it may well be computer games.

In pre-humans and hunter-gatherers, 'games' hardly exist. Certainly there is nothing remotely like organised sport or games with rules. The idea of competitiveness in general tends to be anathema to the level I mind.

While today we take for granted the concept of the 'arts', presupposing that literature, music, painting, drama and many other arts should be taken rather seriously, no such concepts exist among hunter-gatherers, let alone apes. We take it for granted that an appreciation of these arts is a mark of civilisation and a fit use for leisure; that is to say we approve of aesthetics. Such ideas seem to be lacking in hunter-gatherers. This is not to say that painting and engraving, often in a strikingly realistic form, are not found at this level of culture; they definitely are. But they are, on closer inspection, a part of the complex of myth and rites which make up their 'religion'. Similarly dance, song and the use of instruments in music of this level always seem to be intimately bound up with rites and religion.

The sub-divisions of Level I

As we have already noted, the hunter-gatherer level seems to have three main sub-levels, which each cover a much longer time span than any of the higher levels of cultural organisation. No doubt the differences between them are significant, but there is no firm evidence that they are of similar importance to the differences between main levels. Accordingly a brief characterisation of these sub-levels is consigned to appendix B.

The view is taken here that all three belong to a single major culture level, with most features in common. Toolcraft and speech were present in each of them, apparently from the very dawn of humans. Hunting can be seen to be basic to all three sub-levels, and thus the fundamental social unit of the male hunter with the female gatherer and some children is very likely to be present in all of them. In terms of the development of thought, chimps already occupy the highest point of Piaget's first main stage, and surviving hunter-gatherers (of the third sub-level) occupy the very next sub-stage (in Piaget's second main stage of development). There is thus apparently no 'space' in the known development of thought which might have allowed early hunter-gatherers to occupy a more primitive sub-stage than later hunter-gatherers. Since they already had speech, it seems overwhelmingly likely that the earliest hunter-gatherers occupied the same sub-stage of thought as the later hunters of level I, albeit in a simpler form. Because they were evidently at the same broad level of culture, the differences between the three sub-levels were evidently relatively minor.

Level I was by far the longest of the five main levels of culture, and it was the one most different from the level we are familiar with; thus it is appropriate that it should have the longest chapter. We now move to the level of tribal farmers.

Chapter FOUR   THE LEVEL OF TRIBAL FARMERS: Level II (the Neoric)

Section i   **Economy and Technology**

For some time the beginning of farming has been recognised as one of the most important landmarks in human history[1]. The basic idea of agriculture is simple enough, (but it required a great leap of imagination for those who first tried it). It involves the planting and cultivation of food plants. Originally these were selected from wild forms, which soon became semi-domesticated varieties. Continued selection of plants for such qualities as palatibility, nutrition and high yield, led to the domestic varieties, which have survived until recent times.

The beginning of this process of cultivation marks the end of the hunter-gatherer level. Level II proper begins when farming provides the major component of the food supply. Sometimes the process of establishing a farming economy was quite rapid (perhaps less than ten generations), in which case the transitional interlevel (I/II or Mesoric) was quite short. In other situations, the transition was long drawn out, or never completed. Either way, there is always a transitional interlevel[2].

Widely across the Old World, cultivation is accompanied by domestication of animals, to provide meat and other products; hunting became more of an occasional pastime for farmers, instead of the prime source of meat. In the New World by contrast, two of the llama family were the only ungulate animals domesticated, and these were not used much for meat, but mainly for wool and draught. Farming is thus quite possible (and common) without stockraising for food. Rather rarer is herding of animals in a society in which no cultivation is practised. The rare cases of this tend to be from arid or cold regions; (even in these cases, there is often a reciprocal relation with cultivators). Pure pastoralism usually necessitates a nomadic way of life, and is not included in our scheme in level II – the tribal farmers proper[2]. For reasons that are fairly obvious, none of these societies achieved urbanisation.

Farming seems to have been first practised some ten thousand years ago in the near east, where suitable grain-bearing plants were growing wild. Without underestimating for a moment the importance in many cases of the spread of ideas and techniques across human societies, it is vital to realise that both farming and literate civilisation appeared *independently* in several different regions of the world. While wheat and barley were typical of near eastern cultivation, the first farming in China was based on millet, and in the the Americas the principal food crop was maize. Other crops were independently domesticated, such as rice in southeastern or southern Asia.

Whereas hunting is normally a short and simple business of locating and killing prey, cultivation always involves several quite distinct phases, on a single plot, spread out over much of the year. The process may have to start with tree felling and burning, or stone removal. Usually it will then be necessary to prepare the soil, by some activity such as hoeing or ploughing. A better yield can often be obtained by some form of fertilising or manuring. Planting or sowing of seed is the step which all farmers must perform. If there is insufficient rain, watering or localised irrigation may be needed next, and weeding will help improve the yield. Fencing may be necessary to prevent wild or domestic animals from eating or trampling the crop, especially if stock is grazed nearby.

There always has to be some form of harvesting, as this is the object of the exercise. Usually reaping will involve some 'equipment' like a sickle. Finally it is vital to be able to store both the 'seed corn' for the next planting, and the food which will support the community until the next harvest. A skilled farmer will try to replant seed from plants which have been especially good from the point of view of yield, hardiness, nutritiousness or whatever quality seems desirable.

A new feature is that farming provides some real control over the food supply. Of course circumstances may ruin the crop, through exceptional drought or pests for example, but normally the yield is largely under the control of the farmer. Perhaps the most striking single result of the farming economy (even at the simple tribal level) compared to a hunter-gatherer economy, is that the population which can be supported (if conditions are held more or less constant) is about one hundred times as great[3]. This is an increase of nearly ten thousand percent; a relatively empty human world suddenly became much more populated.

A significant consequence of the larger population, and the farming which brought it about, is a greatly increased impact on the environment. Some of the more important processes in this are widespread clearance of woodland, construction of permanent villages, and the effect of intensive grazing.

Another consequence linked to farming is the advent of sedentary living. As we have seen, it is rare for farmers to be able to leave their fields or plots untended for long, as they perform the various seasonal operations we noted above. This means that nomadism is not only unnecessary, it is also impractical or even impossible for those who farm. This is why the first farmers became settled.

While population increase is the most dramatic demographic result of farming, sedentism has other less obvious effects. It seems that the spacing between children falls from about four years in hunting societies to less than three years among farmers. Perhaps mainly for this reason, the average number of children per family also rises. There are also, apparently, modest reductions in premature mortality and increases in life expectancy[3].

The flimsy temporary shelters of the hunter level are no longer needed or suitable. Instead they build permanent houses and farms. Often these are grouped in villages, but the alternative of dispersed homesteads and farms is also quite common. The materials used tend to be much more durable - for example stone or massive hardwood timbers.

Whereas nomadic hunters possess a minimum of equipment and own nothing which is not easily transportable, sedentary farmers (dwelling in permanent houses or huts) can begin to accumulate all sorts of property. This includes things they can not easily carry (or even carry at all). At first there was not a lot of property beyond essentials, but the opportunity to accumulate things tends to grow as time goes on. This in turn leads to the first accumulation of anything that could reasonably be called wealth. Because farmers differ in their skills or luck or intelligence, this is bound to lead to some differential of wealth. At first social mechanisms existed to minimise this, as egalitarianism was still prominent among simple tribal farmers, before the rise of the institution of chiefdoms. Better off people would be under pressure to dissipate their wealth in throwing feasts or giving away or destroying goods; but with time, and the rise of the chiefdom and ranks or classes, the movement is or was towards the accumulation of wealth.

The practice of farming, as we have seen, involves a series of stages, and most of these need equipment or tools. The clearing of woodland requires efficient axes. At first these were mainly of polished stone, but over much of the old world they were later replaced by metal axes – copper and bronze often first, and then iron[4]. Preparing the soil requires something like a spade or hoe or a simple plough; it cannot be done with the bare hands. Containers like baskets or satchels will be needed for carrying seed, and fertilisers, like manure, will need to be collected in containers. Water vessels or runnels will be needed too, if watering is practised. Some sort of sickle or knife will usually be required for harvesting, and perhaps also to make fencing. More containers will be necessary for collecting the harvest.

One of the most characteristic features of tribal farmers is the making of clay pots. Actually these were absent among the earliest farmers of the near east and east mediterranean. Here they used ground stone bowls for two thousand years or so, before pottery was introduced. The ground stone bowls were time consuming to make while pots take only a few minutes, and clay is much more widely available than the high quality stone needed to make stone bowls. Apart from this, pottery was almost universal among tribal farmers. The primary need for pots is probably as a waterproof container for the seed, to keep it dry from harvest time until planting time. Also ceramic bowls are used for domestic tasks like holding water or heating and cooking things. Clay bowls must be fired to make them waterproof.

Another form of craft favoured by tribal farmers is the making of textiles. Thread can be obtained from vegetable sources like flax or cotton, and from animal sources like sheep and alpaca wool. Something like a spindle whorl is often used to prepare the thread. A further set of equipment, for example a loom, is then needed to weave the textile. In tropical regions, the use of certain kinds of bark to make 'bark cloth' is preferred to thread and weaving; here a hammering process, needing a different set of tools, is used. Clothes, as we understand the term, largely replaced the skins and other natural coverings favoured by hunter-gatherers[5].

Sometimes the same equipment used in farming, such as axes, can be used in constructing homes. But often the tools needed in building permanent homes or making furniture would be a different set of carpentry or masonry tools.

A new form of technology appears with the arrival of primitive warfare. Previously hunter-gatherers seem to have used the same weapons for fighting that they used in hunting. But tribal farmers engage in something which can already be called war, although only on a small scale and for brief periods. Arms made specially for war in level II include maces or battle axes, daggers and rapiers and war spears. Special equipment to protect the body in combat is still rare or unknown, but simple shields are occasionally found.

There are two more new developments among tribal farmers. The first is the dawn of craft specialisation, which may be detected in any of the new types of technology – ceramics, building, textiles or war for example. However it remains small scale and rare. Most people are still engaged in farming, and things like textiles and pottery would be mainly produced as part time activities, when the needs of farming were less pressing.

The second new development is linked to the beginning of craft specialisation and to the small surpluses mentioned above. It is the beginning of small scale and local trade. Such a 'balanced' trade, recognising value, is extremely rare in hunter-gatherer society, (though various kinds of gift giving, and chains of exchange are known). Trade in level II is necessarily mainly by barter, for coinage and weights of precious metal are not yet in use. Markets become commoner, as chiefdoms begin to become established, and the concept of market value of objects or commodities begins to arise.

Section ii   **Social and Political Organisation**

Among hunter-gatherers, as we have seen, the local 'band' is the most basic unit, and it usually numbers only some twenty-five to thirty persons. Although the structure of such a community is very loose, it does tend to act in a concerted way, when necessary. It is the largest group so to do. By contrast among tribal farmers, a much larger group has some political cohesion. This is the tribe which usually numbers in thousands or tens of thousands.

It is likely that the farming tribe evolves out of the hunter-gatherer 'paleo-tribe'; both sorts of tribe have a shared language or dialect, while outsiders tend to speak a different tongue. The much larger size of the true tribe is easily explained by the massive population increase which occurs between hunters and tribal farmers – an increase, as we saw, of about one hundred times. Thus if a paleo-tribe usually has about five to six hundred persons, and this is increased by a hundred times, the result will be of the order of fifty thousand persons. Often the territory is of much the same general size. In other cases, the territory can be larger, and thus a tribal size of hundreds of thousands is also sometimes found.

Among the tribal farmers, the strongest social bonds are to be found in the smaller units like the family, the village or local clan. Above were all sorts of possible groupings or segments – sections, moieties, age-grades, major clans, sub-tribes and so on. The highest grouping is the tribe, and this is the level at which cohesion is least strong, and perhaps only intermittent[6].

Whereas the paleo-tribe had no leader, and the band only an informal or honorary headman with no real power, the tribe, and its smaller segments, tend to have leaders with some real power. In many cases this led in time to an even stronger figure – a chief, (who is the characteristic feature of the second or higher sub-level of level II). An additional focus of power in the level II tribe is a council of elders. Normally the tribal leader or chief tries to work in collaboration with both the council and with the local leaders. 'Government' of a centralised kind does not exist at this tribal level.

Hunter-gatherers do not recognise ownership of land, either by individuals or by the band. The most they recognise is a right to any game or other food taken by their own effort. The band, and to some extent the paleo-tribe, do have a territory, which they will try to defend from encroachment. By contrast, farmers claim ownership of their land. They would assume that it was right to defend it against outsiders, and the tribe would co-operate, if necessary, to help local communities or villages to protect themselves or their land.

As we saw in the previous section, the tendency to accumulate modest surpluses and 'wealth' is always present in farming societies, and thus the tendency for there to arise a differential of wealth is a social as well as an economic phenomenon. The growth of 'craft' specialisation and new occupations, such as that of priest, is also eroding the egalitarian ethos inherited from hunter-gatherers. For example, among african tribes, the iron smiths are or were a separate itinerant caste, despised by the tribespeople. It is common for accomplished warriors, even if only 'part time', to be regarded as of higher status than ordinary farmers. Slaves are rare in early tribal society[7], but become more typical in tribal chiefdoms, of later level II. (They are universal in the succeeding level III.) It is hard for egalitarianism to flourish in a slave-holding society. As a result of these factors, the society of tribal chiefdoms tends to be 'ranked' in an informal hierarchy.

Violence and killing are quite common in hunter-gatherer societies. But the term war is inappropriate before tribal farmers, who practise it on a small scale, often between tribes or segments of them. Hunters used the same spears and arrows for killing humans that they used when hunting game. But as we saw in our discussion of technology, tribal farmers already have special weapons for conflict; and for the first time there are specialist warriors. Tribal farmers also construct simple defences, such a bank and ditch, with or without a palisade.

Section iii **Numeracy, Thought and Religion**

In the field of number words, a clear difference between hunters and farmers emerges[8]. Hunter-gatherers employ (in addition to a simple formula of words for one, two and many) a count based on two; (alternatively one could say this is not really a number at all, but more the notion of a pair or duo). An additive two count goes:- one, two, two+one, two+two, two+two+one and so on. Counting significantly above ten was thus extremely difficult, but body and finger counts were also used. Some hunters use a multiplicative system of low numbers words, but this rarely goes as high as five times two. Written numbers were of course unknown.

By contrast tribal farmers rarely use a two count, but instead use number words of a system with five and ten as bases (or sometimes five and twenty)[8]. A five-ten count goes:- one, two, three, four, *five*, five+one, five+two, five+three, five+four, *ten*, ten+one, ten+two, ten+three, ten+four, *ten+five*, ten+five+one, and so on. With this sort of system, it is possible but cumbersome to count up to fifty or more. Again written numbers are unknown.

The 'two system' has an echo in mythic thought. In hunter-gatherer myths, great emphasis is placed on 'two' or 'pair'. Again and again a **pair** of characters are prominent in the story, but higher numbers are rarely used. Two seems to be a kind of magic or special number. Tribal farmers' myth employs two no more than higher number words. These include four, seven, ten and twelve, all of which have some form of sacred significance for one tribe or another.

A second feature in which hunter-gatherer mythic narrative is different from that of farmers is the way in which the main characters (mythic ancestors) are presented as hunting or foraging as they wander across their land, (just like the people who recount their myths). By the time of tribal farmers, we no longer find major characters depicted as hunting and wandering, (nor even usually as farming).

The next important difference is that the mythic thought of tribal farmers includes strong indications of the idea of gods, or rather emergent gods. There is for example often a word for a 'god'. Nothing comparable is found in hunter-gatherer myth or thought. The significance of this development runs deeper, as we shall see below, in connection with the decline of the egalitarian ethos.

A further important difference concerns myths of death, where two distinctive mythic motifs are widely found in level II, in place of the rather confused and vague ideas of death, typical of hunter-gatherers. (Because for the latter, the spirit is the 'real' person, a dead body does not fully mean 'death'. The spirit is still alive; and characters in myths are always resurrecting. So in a sense, death does not exist.)

The first of the two tribal farmer motifs is the 'mortality-a-mishap' theme. According to this, previously people never fully died; (perhaps this harks back to the level I ideas). However, due to some mishap or accident, the situation changed, and death became definitive or final.

The second death motif is the 'death-to-life' theme. According to this idea, a death can make a useful contribution, because it leads (in some vague and unspecified way) to fruitfulness and new life. Farmers know that plants tend to die down, and to be 'reborn' or to give off the seeds of new life; and this would obviously suggest some such idea. This death motif has an important, if grisly, consequence, because it leads to the rite of sacrifice. "If death promotes new fertility, why not help it along by means of rites of killing?" In level II, tribal farmers begin to sacrifice animals and humans. (Human sacrifice reaches its climax in the succeeding level – archaic literate states. Then during the fourth level human sacrifice, and later animal sacrifice, go out of fashion. In the fifth level, the idea provokes horror.)

Tribal farmers regularly adhere to five mythic ideas on the main features of their universe. These are found in all the main regions where tribal peoples survived to recent times, but were absent among all hunter-gatherers (with one possible but dubious exception[9]). The idea of an <u>earth mother</u> is not found in any hunter-gatherer peoples, but is widely found in tribal farmers. It is of course obvious that the idea of the 'earth' or soil being a primal deity and a fertility goddess or 'mother of all', would be likely to appeal to primitive farmers.

Secondly tribal farmers are inclined to see their world as a <u>giant spheroid.</u> For some it was a giant egg, for others a gourd, and for others a kind of shell or double shell, like a clam. The upper half is the sky vault or sky father. The lower half is where the earth and the waters are sited. Sometimes this is the earth mother, sometimes just the earth floating in a sea in a bowl.

Following on from the 'spheroid' concept is the idea that originally the sky was very low, and in some heroic <u>sky lift</u>, it was heaved up to its present position, so that people could have some more headroom. These ideas are surprisingly widespread, being found in tribal farmers of Africa, Oceania, America and Asia. (Europe of course has no proper ethnographic record of this level.)

Then there are mythic ideas about the two great luminaries. Tribal farmers' ideas are similar to those held in more recent levels. The <u>sun</u> is a major power or deity; it is almost always seen as <u>male</u>, and it is a benefactor to man, which should be revered. The <u>moon</u> is less important, usually seen as <u>female</u>, and less beneficial to mankind.

The picture of these features in hunter-gatherer thought is quite different. The earth mother idea is quite absent, as is the cosmic spheroid. The remaining three cosmographic ideas are different across the whole hunter sample (but see note 9); thus the sky lift idea is not a level I idea. Surprisingly the sun and moon are seen quite differently. Among hunter-gatherers the moon is routinely regarded as more important and beneficial than the sun; and it is almost always a male figure. By contrast, the sun is usually female for hunters, relatively rarely mentioned in myth, and on those occasions usually seen as harmful or inconvenient.

There is a further change in mythic ideas, which concerns origins. According to hunter-gatherers, the ancestors 'presided' over some simple events, often the origin of a single tree or river, usually unplanned or by accident. Tribal farmers have a quite different sort of account of origins, which can reasonably be called a simple creation story. They include ideas like 'primal nothingness or void', a series of creations of classes of things or animals, and the idea of creation by command. All these are lacking in hunters.

Before moving on to the four founding principles of mythic thought, we may reiterate that the concentration on mythic thought is justified, because there was litle in the thought of either hunter-gatherers or tribal farmers which was not overtly mythic or imbued with myth.

The mythic and social principle of egalitatianism (across the whole spectrum from rocks to ancestors), which we saw was so typical of hunter-gatherers, disappears entirely during the period of tribal farmers, and the first signs of this demise are apparent as soon as farming is well established. We noted above that the emergence of 'gods' is obviously related to this development. Similarly as farmers no longer see mountains or rivers or similar inanimate objects as alive, the principle of pan-animism becomes severely modified, and is restricted increasingly to animals or humans. Then the extremely simple idea of a 'sacred bond' uniting all phenomena is quickly changed. Religious ideas become more complex, and above all more focussed and discriminating. Tribal farming societies were no longer satisfied with the vague kind of feelings and emotions of the preceding level.

The simple concept of manipulating or tricking spirits by 'magic' changes in level II. Even more importantly, the role of the practitioner of magic, the shaman, alters by becoming more diversified. For hunter-gatherers the shaman is the only kind of person with a special 'religious' role. He or she is strictly amateur, being obliged to procure food along with the rest, and there is basically only one role involved.

The more complex world of tribal farmers has a quite new disposition of religious roles. The first big change is the emergence of the priest, whose prime role is to officiate in public rites and ceremonies. He tends to be a rather different kind of personality from the preceding shaman, who was often reserved, prone to trances and disinclined to perform before a large congregation. The priest needs to be impressive, with a good voice and charismatic manner. (Priestesses were rarer, but in later levels acquired a role of their own).

The shamanic functions did not cease to exist with the arrival of priests. On the contrary, these roles are diversified. A distinction comes to be made between the healer (witch-doctor or medicine-man) and a more sinister figure (sorcerer or witch) who causes illness, perhaps on behalf of a client with a grudge[10]. Another shaman-like role is the foretelling of the future; this is a largely new idea, because previously hunter-gatherers had little notion of, or interest in, the future. These new diviners or seers use a wide variety of techniques[11]. Finally there is now room in some tribal societies for a 'medium' or spiritualist, whose 'necromancy' puts people in touch with the dead, and for a rainmaker, who may assume considerable importance for farmers, if drought becomes a problem.

With the new farming economy, and farming myths, emerge new rites appropriate for tribal farmers. Where hunters already had very basic 'life crisis' rites (birth, puberty, marriage and death) which could vary from elaborate to very peremptory, the tribal farmers have seasonal rites. The most typical are usually 'rogations' at planting time (asking for a good harvest), and a 'harvest festival' (giving thanks for a successful harvest). A related development is the beginning of the creation of a calendar. Hunter-gatherers are aware of the seasons, but do not have even the most elementary system of days in a calendar year. For practical reasons to do with their farming, but probably even more so to do with the seasonal rites, tribal farmers begin to develop calendars which predict some of the more important markers (such as midsummer and midwinter). As we shall see, this was to become much more formalised in the succeeding level. Calendrics was probably the first ever quantitative skill.

Another new feature of primarily religious importance is the construction of more permanent focuses of worship, such as temples or shrines, instead of the natural places used by hunters. Similarly we find burial monuments, which survived to be visible to posterity. This is an aspect of tribal farmers, which is almost as obvious from archaeological evidence as it is from ethnographic reports.

<u>The tribal farmer thought level</u>

It is appropriate to stress once more that our reconstruction of the two levels discussed so far is in no way based on a preconceived assumption that their thought must fit with the stages of mental development made famous by Jean Piaget. But it is instructive to note that the picture obtained from direct evidence does in fact fit well with Piaget's stages.

In this chapter we are concerned primarily with Piaget's sub-stage IIb of child thought, the 'intuitive' mode (see note 23 of the preceding chapter). The first point to note about this intuitive sub-stage, and its contrast with the preceding sub-stage, is that 'artificialistic' explanations are in the ascendancy over animistic notions. Let us take the example of a cloud that moves. A child of the pre-conceptual sub-stage (IIa) will say that the cloud moves itself or is alive; this animistic explanation posits a spirit or will inherent in the cloud. A child of the intuitive sub-stage (IIb), by contrast, will say that 'someone' is moving the cloud. The mover is personalised; if the subject is familiar with the concept of deities, he or she will say that the mover is 'a god'. These two ways of thinking almost exactly replicate the two ways of looking at the problem found in hunter-gatherers and tribal farmers. Generally the level I view is that the will or spirit in a thing makes it move. The level II view is that a thing is moved by a force which is personalised; this will usually be an emergent deity, who will be credited with 'powers' or the ability to control things.

This brings us on to a second feature of Piagetian 'intuitive' thought – an elementary concept of a world that is ordered, and the idea that events are caused. Cause and effect are absent from hunter-gatherer thought, but 'gods' are conceived as having the ability to cause or change events according to tribal farmer thought..

In the intuitive sub-stage, games which imitate reality tend to replace games of pure pretence. This seems to be mirrored in the difference between hunter-gatherer rituals and those of tribal farmers. Level I rituals seem to be almost exclusively imaginative, whereas level II ritual seems to re-enact phenomena seen as important. We have already noted the rite of sacrifice, which re-enacts part of the cycle of death and re-birth.

A fourth feature of intuitive thought is the way that it exhibits less violation of proportionality or realism than found in the pre-conceptual thought from which it develops. As it happens violation of proportionality is rather typical of level I or hunter-gatherer thought. For example we noted an australian aboriginal story of a hunter who receives a severe cut on the head, and blood spurts out. Soon it fills the valley, and everyone is drowned. Although this kind of thinking is common in level I myth, it seems that the myth and thought of tribal farmers has less tendency to lack a sense of proportionality and more of a tendency to 'realism'.

There are three further features of intuitive thought which together find echoes in level II thinking:- the arrival of elementary concrete concepts[12]; some progress in de-centration; and a decline in egocentricity. We saw in chapter three that centration is typical of the pre-conceptual sub-stage, and level I thought; it is a kind of one track mind, in which more than one feature can never be considered at a time. As such it accounts for the routine tolerance of inconsistencies and contradictions, found in level I myths. With de-centration, the inconsistencies begin to worry the subject. This seems to be already appearing in level II societies, where the more blatant examples have been replaced.

Egocentricity meant for Piaget, as we saw in the preceding chapter, the inability to see anything from any other point of view than one's own. Level I religion was prone to this sort of thing; for example 'good' and 'bad' tends to be seen stictly from a personal point of view; and again the 'sacred bond' was apparently between an individual and the whole undifferentiated cosmos. Among tribal farmers, religion and worship are concerned with the needs of the wider community; their more excessive egocentricity seems to have been curbed.

As far as the concepts of 'leisure and aesthetics' are concerned, these seem still to be absent in tribal farmers. The art of level II is typically more stylised than that of level I, and it is no longer dominated by animals. Where scenes in a recognisable form were absent in level I, they are apparently sometimes present in level II. It is always difficult to recognise and interpret mythic stories from primitive art, unless one already knows the story, but perhaps it has become a little easier in tribal farmers' art.

Chapter FIVE   THE LEVEL OF ARCHAIC LITERATE STATES: Level III

Section i **Social, Political and Military Organisation**

The level of tribal farmers ends when the formation of a state occurs[1]. The differences between the state and tribal organisation are very marked. This change is of the same kind of importance as the beginnings of toolcraft and farming, (which as we have seen defined, successively, the start of the two preceding levels). The state has a single supreme ruling authority, which may also be said to constitute 'true' government. In the preceding level of tribal farmers, there is no single supreme ruling authority, either in theory or in practice. Even the head of a strong tribal chiefdom lacks supreme power[2]. In tribal farming societies, there is no centralised power. The leader or chief has modest powers or influence, but often some kind of council of elders has similar or greater influence.

Membership of a tribe is defined by kinship, even though this may be partly fictitious. The state (and membership of it) is defined by territory; it is the area over which governance has been imposed. Everyone in the territory is subject to the state, (except possibly ambassadors and visitors, and they would have to be careful to abide by the rules of the state, if required). We also need to note that the form of the state can vary a lot. But there are basically only two main types:- the city state, as found among the Sumerians, the Maya and the Greeks for example; and the empire, as for example the Akkadian and Babylonian empires of Mesopotamia, and the Chinese dynastic empires. A city state may acquire an empire.

When the state comes into being, its government (at least in theory) assumes total power. Once this has been done, it then delegates this power back to officials. These might be central government officials, or regional governors, or some other kind of functionaries, like priests. All of these officials can be dismissed by the same central authority which has appointed them. The state has a monopoly of power, and of the use of force, whereas tribes have no such monopoly.

Typically the single ruling authority is a monarch, and thus the normal form of government of archaic literate states is an autocratic monarchy. Usually the monarch is male, but a female 'king' or 'queen' may rule from time to time. I am unaware of any archaic literate state of level III where an 'oligarchy' or 'aristocracy' ruled officially. The nominal ruler can of course be weak or a puppet, in which case real power is exercised through the monarch by a chief minister or 'vizier' or perhaps a group of officials. It is usually taken for granted that a dynasty of monarchs, with descent passing to sons (or less often daughters or other close relatives), is the 'correct' form of rulership. Thus a weak monarch will not always lead to an end of monarchy, for often stronger heirs will restore the rule without the dynasty collapsing.

As we shall see, dynastic states of this kind are prone to collapse. Sometimes this is total, other times only partial. Sometimes a new dynasty or a nearby civilisation restores the situation locally. Sometimes limited use of the script survives, and sometimes other elements of the civilisation continue. However the full panoply of state rule rarely survived intact for more than five hundred years. Often this was due to military overthrow, but the reasons are not always clear[3].

In literate states, it is normal for a law code to be drafted, and to be displayed in public. As we shall see in section iii, ability to read and write is the preserve of only a tiny minority, but no doubt the state always found a way to proclaim the laws to those who could not read. At this level, laws and punishments are usually harsh by modern western standards. For those who get on the wrong side of the state, savage torture and executions are common, and are regarded by the people as normal. A state or royal guard would act as a police force when necessary, operating primarily in the interests of the ruler and state. A network of informers and spies would also often exist.

By contrast, laws (especially written laws) are unknown among tribal farmers, and although killings and feuds are common, execution, imprisonment and torture are not typical institutions in a tribal society. This is much as one would expect, where kin relations continue to be important. The family and local or kin groups remain in early states, but they no longer enjoy the kind of autonomy or influence they had in tribal times.

Another very significant innovation in archaic literate states is the emergence of a rigid class system. A typical hierarchy includes six or more classes, such as royals, nobles, higher officials, lower officials, farmers, traders and craftsmen, and labourers or peasants. In addition, all known archaic literate states have slavery[4], usually resulting from the enslavement of conquered neighbours. Slaves often make up a sizeable portion of the population in level III, and constitute the lowest class. By contrast, among hunter-gatherers and early tribal farmers[5], no trace of a formal class system is found, and they tend to be egalitarian[5].

The main change in the nature of the family is to be found in the higher classes. Here higher status men regularly take a number of wives, and often concubines also. This results in large households which include servants and slaves, and are notably different from anything which had existed hitherto. Among the lower classes the family continues much as before, but larger kinship groups, such as clans, tend to diminish in importance or disappear. A further social difference stems from the increase in settlement size. Towns become normal, and the capital 'cities' are often huge. As a result a substantial portion of the population are now town dwellers, whereas previously the vast majority had been rural or village dwellers. A new urban 'proletariat' emerges. The demographic results of the above factors are significant. The archaic state regularly has a population of over a million, and larger capital cities also have a million or more people. Some improved medical expertise develops, but it was usually available only to the higher classes. Conditions in towns tend to be less healthy for the lower classes than those in the countryside. Thus there is only a modest demographic improvement. Premature mortality falls slightly, and the expectation of life seems to increase a little. It still averages only in the order of about thirty-five years, even for those who have survived beyond fifteen years of age[6].

The difference between the habitations of the poor and rich is considerable. The highest classes would have elegant town houses or palaces, often with gardens, while the lower classes would presumably have lived in small or cramped dwellings. Similarly the clothes of the rich would be better made, and more 'fashionable' than ever before. It is doubtful if the rural lower classes were any worse off than their predecessors had been. In post-tribal society, their poverty may have been no more than relative.

There are further differences in the field of hostilities and war. For the first time large scale war was practised. Indeed many early civilisations seem to have come into existence as a result of it. The state with its monopoly of 'legitimate' force keeps armies, at least intermittently, and usually permanently. There are professional officers and generals, and at least some of the soldiers are professional. All the soldiers will receive some kind of remuneration, even if it is only their keep. There will be some kind of uniform and helmet, as well as a shield and standardised arms.

Because the economic infrastructure is strong enough to support them, prolonged campaigns can be fought. To counter the danger of the state being attacked, fortifications will be built, with walls of dressed stone or brick, and towers and gates.

If states erect fortifications, techniques of siegecraft are likely to be developed in response.

Section ii **Economy and Technology**

Superficially, the main economy of early states is based on the same kind of simple farming techniques, which had been used by tribal farmers. But there are important differences, notably the undertaking of large scale hydraulic or other infrastructure projects. The most obvious of these is irrigation, which often increases the yield of crops by many times. To be effective, the works need to be on a large scale, bringing water from as high and plentiful a supply as possible, and channelling it in a systematic way to irrigate as large a cultivated area as possible. The success of this was such that population at this level is regularly two to four times as high as that found in tribal farmers in similar circumstances[7]. Only with centralised direction and organisation are such projects possible.

Of equal importance is flood defence. It has been estimated that in the long run, large scale flood defence has more effect by saving crops or villages, than the irrigation itself[8]; it allowed a continuing large population to survive in areas prone to flooding. A similar project is channelling water for drinking, and other household needs, to areas with large populations. In some low lying areas, the land is too wet for for easy cultivation, and drainage projects can ensure unflooded fields with adjacent channels or dykes from which water can be transferred easily to irrigate crops.

A parallel and partly related development, is the improvement of long distance transport. In many ancient civilisations, road construction is indicated; sometimes roads are crudely paved. But for many early states, water provides a more convenient avenue of transport. Rivers are used or 'improved'. Canals constructed specially, or as an adjunct to agriculture, become major transport routes. In connection with this, boats are improved or built larger, and heavy loads can be for the first time transported. All this is without close parallel in the culture of tribal farmers[9].

The economy changes with the advent of the state and literacy. Many more people are engaged in work other than the production of food. For hunter-gatherers, the food quest involved over 99% of the able population, and for tribal farmers it was still probably over 90%. But as cities and craft activities expanded, the proportion falls significantly. There are many more craft specialisations, and many more people engaged in them. Partly as a result, trade increases sharply. (But it was held back by the absence of a convenient and suitable currency. It was still necessary to use barter or something like inconvenient currency bars.) The increased production of food, due to irrigation and other advances, and of goods made by artisans, leads to substantial surpluses and a great increase in the total of wealth (even of *per capita* wealth), compared to the previous level.

The state has control of this new kind of economy and its surpluses. State officials assume responsibility for distributing much of the goods. In the case of state controlled agriculture, all the produce belongs in the first instance to the state, and farmers and labourers will be given some of the food for subsistence and reward. At the other end of the scale, in remote and unproductive areas, subsistence farming would have continued almost unchanged, (but no doubt local officials kept a sharp eye open for signs of sufficient surplus to make it possible to 'tax' it.) It is for this sort of reason that many level III states are known to have conducted censuses of their population, and recorded the results in documents.

In this new kind of 'redistributive' economy, the state owns or controls most of the land and the production. Where production is still private, the state will endeavour to tax it in some way, but in the absence of money this will have to be in the form of levies or a share of the produce. The state, sometimes by means of the temple and priesthood, will store large reserves, some of which will be needed to feed those workers not engaged in food production. A bad harvest, and especially a series of bad harvests, will nevertheless still often lead to famine.

An alternative to taxation is to draft workers, not immediately needed in farming, onto state projects. These 'corvees' are needed for various purposes, notably the infrastructure projects (like irrigation), but perhaps most significantly they are used for 'prestige projects'. It is apparently universally the case that ancient states and empires construct large-scale impressive buildings and monuments. These can be temples, town walls or gateways, palaces or tombs. One should not minimise such pre-level III monuments as Stonehenge, Great Zimbabwe or the Maltese temples, thought to have been erected by tribal farmers (but just possibly resulting from the influence of early states); but the fact is that the great structures of literate states (for example in Egypt, Mesopotamia, China or Mexico) are of an entirely different order from anything produced by tribal farmers. The finer state buildings are made of dressed masonry or brick or similar advanced building materials, having extensive roofed areas and elaborate doors and windows. Often they had monumental decorative carving as well.

We have noted, above, the large hydraulic projects; these require greater technical knowledge, skill and organisation than any level II achievements. Similarly the new buildings and monuments necessitate more advanced skills, like quarrying and accurate stone dressing, as well as architectural expertise and the use of newly available surveying skills and the mathematics involved in them.

The technology of ancient states also seems to include, for the first time, simple 'machines'. Examples are the shaduf and the sakhia[10], used in the near east. This new level of technology is clearly higher than the primitive technology of hunter-gatherers and tribal farmers. It can perhaps legitimately be called intermediate technology.

Craft activities, as we have seen, increase markedly in early states, and involve a much larger number of people. In some cases such as the production of household ceramic pots, this is achieved by pioneer 'mass production', possibly using machines, (but without of course powered machinery). Craft specialisation is an important factor in boosting trade in level III. Apparently this more intensive trading was regularly encouraged by early literate states, which often controlled or taxed these activities. For the first time, some of the trade is over long distances, between provinces or separate states. At this level there is the opportunity for merchants to emerge as a class, and to acquire considerable wealth, but their status in the class system usually remains low.

The new upper class and their wealth encourage, wittingly or unwittingly, the production (or extraction) of luxury goods and commodities. In some areas metals, like gold and silver, acquire high value, and can be used as a form of currency, especially when standard weights have come into use. Other products like fabrics, ivory or scents come to be valued, and assume the status of a kind of money. It is reasonably certain that large markets (like soukhs) are regularly in existence in states of level III.

The first farmers made a considerable impact on the natural environment, by felling large areas of woodland. Now in level III with the growth of cities and with the large scale infrastructure projects we noted above, this impact is greatly increased. Much of the heartland of these ancient states is transformed, and large areas of natural environment are lost. There is little realisation of the significance of what is happening; a normal attitude is that man, or at least the rulers, have been given dominion over nature.

Section iii   **Communication, Religion and Thought**

The invention of a script, and the beginning of true writing, mark an obvious step forward. Literacy is present, by definition, in all level III states, and writing is destined to become of outstanding importance. Hunters and tribal farmers lacked writing, and had only verbal language. 'Ideas' had to be remembered and passed on verbally, typically as myth. It is generally difficult to examine and consider ideas objectively if they are not written down, and thus writing is an important step along the road that leads to a more systematic and rational form of thought[11].

Only a small section of the population in level III states is able to read or write. 'Scribes' are a necessary and influential section of the upper tiers of level III society. A few of them may have acquired considerable learning. One of the duties of scribes is to keep records. Quite a few of these have survived from thousands of years ago. In addition to rather dry lists of food and commodities stored, many other things were noted down. Censuses were apparently quite common, but few of these survive.

In every case where we have good information, written numbers were introduced at the same time as written words, (though in theory they could have been introduced earlier or later). These number ciphers greatly aid the emergence of practical mathematics, (which was, as we saw, of great value in improving surveying and architectural skills). The use of much larger numbers now becomes routine; figures in thousands or tens of thousand can be recorded easily, if needed. Standardised weights and measures are also introduced at this time, and they contribute to practical and commercial advances – the use of standard weights of metal in trade, for example.

As with the origins of agriculture, it is clear that states and literacy emerged independently in many areas. The scripts are quite different in Mesopotamia, Egypt, China, Mexico, the Indus valley and Mycenean Greece. A single invention of script, and its subsequent diffusion to all other areas is clearly not consistent with the facts.

A further new development is the writing down of myth, which provides us with samples of myths from this level, often thousands of years old. As a result of script, written myth begins to acquire a literary or even epic status. Here we are in the realm of the religion of archaic literate states. (It is likely that a genuinely secular outlook on life still does not exist at this level. All thought is still imbued with mythic concepts, and according to Frankfort still personalised.) Religion is harnessed to the needs of the archaic state, and to the promotion of its ruler. An ancient idea of monarchy is that "the king and the land are one".

In archaic states, we find for the first time that religion begins to operate on two or more tiers or levels. The peasants, and the lower orders in general, continue with a folk religion that still has a lot in common with that of tribal farmers. The ruling classes with their priests and scholars are in the process of elaborating a more elevated state religion. This division into tiers of religion reflects the division found in the social order itself, into the classes of a lower tier and those of a higher tier (which includes the literate, some more gifted individuals and the ruling élite). The lower tier, who retained a kind of folk religion, will be left in no doubt that it is the higher tier of religion which really matters, and that they would have to accept the state religion and its values, whenever required to.

State religions of level III are polytheistic, and the gods in question are no longer 'emergent', but are full-blown and elevated. Religions tend to mirror the society they serve. The early state had a very obvious hierarchy from the ruler down through higher officials to lower officials and various classes below these. In a similar way we find the pantheon of gods has a ruler (or supreme god) and a division between more important gods and lesser gods, down to figures like local or household gods, who are hardly gods at all. By this time, all trace of the egalitarian ethos typical of hunter-gatherers has disappeared, both in the realm of mythic thought and in society.

Not only is the earthly ruler mirrored by a supreme god, in level III. He is also often personally regarded as divine or semi-divine, but the form this takes varies from one civilisation to another. In Egypt all pharaohs are automatically 'son of Ra' and thus divine, while in Mesopotamia there are only a few indications of the ruler being divine. In China and Japan, we find the emperors are unquestionably divine.

As the gods become more elevated, so their temples have to be larger and more magnificent. Unlike the shrines or small 'temples' of the tribal farmers, they will be roofed, and enclosed by doors or screening walls. Probably only priests or priestly rulers will be allowed to enter. Priests will now be more numerous and fully professional. They will have a hierarchy, like the society they serve, with chief priests at the top. The ruler may be seen as the highest priest. The stories of the elevated gods become more conceptualised, assuming epic proportions. They become more 'formalised', aided by the standardising effect of writing.

We saw that among tribal farmers, typical ceremonies included the life crisis rites and seasonal agricultural rites. More spectacular ceremonies emerge in states of level III, concerning for example the accession or coronation of a ruler, and in due course the ruler's death and funeral. The major gods will also be celebrated in grand ceremonies.

There were already a variety of forms of divination in tribal farming society, many of which continue into level III; and there was an elementary grasp of the calender. However what is new in level III is a system of astrology, using the movements of the planets. This was not found in the preceding level, where often instead of recognising the planet venus, they still imagined that the morning star and the evening star were different bodies. It seems that all known archaic literate states possess a knowledge of the planets and constellations, and practise astrology on the basis of this, (though not necessarily using the divisions of the zodiac we are familiar with). State or royal astrologers become necessary and influential, and the systematic observation of the skies which this demands becomes, in the course of time, the basis of astronomy, the 'pathfinder' science of the later levels.

Because the state is intolerant of competition, and because higher tier religion now above all promotes the state and the ruler, religions tend to become more exclusive and intolerant as well. From this slowly emerges the idea, hitherto unknown, that different religions are somehow incompatible. If you practise one, you should not also belong to another.

The connection between morality and religion was for most of human history a grey area. Custom was the prime guide to morality and correct behaviour. The advent of law codes in level III adds a new dimension, but only in later levels does the idea emerge that morality might be something beyond custom and the law.

As with society and religion, so with the level of thought, we must make a distinction between what happens in the higher tiers and the lower tiers of the population. In level III, the latter continue to think in much the same way as they had in the previous level. As we have seen, this was at Piaget's 'intuitive' sub-stage of thinking. The prime indication of moving beyond this mode of thought to the next stage – concrete operational thought – is the ability called by Piaget 'conservation'. [A classic test of conservation uses two identical beakers with an equal measure of coloured liquid in each. One beaker is then poured into a taller narrower beaker. A child of the intuitive sub-stage usually says that the taller beaker now has more liquid than the other. By contrast a child who has reached Piaget stage III (the concrete operational) says correctly that both still have the same amount, **and** can give a more or less sensible explanation of why.]

For the more educated and professional classes in early states, and especially in the case of anyone with technical and mathematical skills, it seems likely that they would be able to pass conservation tests successfully. The same people would probably also pass another practical test, which involves classification into sets and subsets, realising that items can belong both to a set and to a subset. There are two further related 'concrete operational' achievements:- the ability to work with a group of separate variables; (this is complete de-centration in Piaget's terminology); and the full rejection of an 'egocentric' view of the world – (this involves being able to see things from numerous different points of view). All these would add up to a much more effective ability to discriminate different things or phenomena (for example into various cross cutting classes). These are the sort of mental skills that an architect or planner would need in the major construction works typically undertaken by a complex level III state.

Lastly we may turn to the 'extra sector' of games, leisure and aesthetics. We have seen that games with rules, and formalised leisure activities were not found in hunter-gatherers, and probably not in tribal societies. With the early civilisations of level III this changes, but probably almost exclusively for people in the higher classes of society. Certainly board games exist, presumably with rules. Also leisure pursuits (ironically mainly in the form of hunting, which had been almost the sole 'work' in level I) are now favoured by the ruling classes. The situation regarding team games with rules is less clear. In the case of the Maya ball court games, it is thought that these were dominantly 'religious', and the winning team were sacrificed! This is a long way from western ideas of sport, but also a clear step beyond anything found in the lower culture levels.

The ruling class and the rich in early civilisations not only have the possibility of leisure, but could also commission 'works of art', and there is little doubt that a dawning concept of aesthetics is already present at this level. The 'artists' themselves at this level are almost invariably anonymous. Clearly at level III, ideas of art and games are very different from modern western ideas, and from primitive ideas.

In a more general way, we may sum up this chapter by saying that we have reviewed a whole range of features in which this level of archaic literate states differs from the preceding levels, and differs as we shall see from the culture levels which follow.

Chapter SIX   THE LEVEL OF PIONEER RATIONALITY: Level IV, the Novaric
(Greco-Roman and Medieval Civilisation)

This level is treated in two parts. In the first we treat the transition from level III to
level IV (that is, the proto-Novaric interlevel) and the first sub-level (technically the
Alpha-Novaric), but also a series of generalisations, which apply to the whole of this
level of pioneer 'rationality-based' states.   The second sub-level – 'medieval'
civilisation (or more technically the Beta-Novaric) is sufficiently different that it
requires extensive separate treatment, and this forms part two of the chapter.

Part One   The transition to and early part of level IV

Section i   **Communication and Thought**

The invention of a phonetic script, which defines the start of the Proto-Novaric.

Some time before 700 B.C., people in the greek world took the semitic consonantal
'alphabet' and transformed it into a true phonetic alphabet with vowels[1].   This
innovation is used here to mark the end of the preceding level of cultural organisation,
level III of archaic literate states (or the Gramoric). It is clear that the new script is
based on the twenty two consonantal letters of the phoenician or canaanite script,
because the greeks use the same signs, barely modified, in the same order, and called
them by names which are only slightly different from those used in the east
Mediterranean.

The modification is accomplished by changing five of the letters from consonants to
vowels, and adding five new letters[2]. The vowels are basically the same as the five
short vowels used in present western script, because we use the roman script, which is
derived from the greek one; there are also two long vowels in the greek script.
(Probably even from the start, the plan to make the script consistently phonetic was
only partially successful. With modifications of the greek language, and problems of
transferring the alphabet to other languages, it became increasingly flawed.) In spite
of such problems, it led to a far higher level of literacy than had been achieved in any
of the preceding states, where only a tiny élite could read and write. There is little
doubt that all subsequent societies using an alphabet have a much easier time in
establishing literacy than those who did not. Accurate figures for the literacy rate in
the greek world are not available, but it is probable that well over half of the free male
citizenry could, at the height of hellenic civilisation, read and write adequately.

Some time during the sixth or fifth century B.C., 'knowledge' begins for the first time to be written down, and educated people could often gain access to it without too much difficulty. The process remains a two tier affair. Most slaves, women and some other less privileged persons did not have much opportunity to participate in this 'learning' in the greco-roman world.

The Dawn of Rationality

The major advance in rational thought, which defines the new level of cultural organisation, level IV, is accomplished by about 550 B.C., also in the greek world. It is doubtful if it would have been possible without widespread literacy. Whether it is in any sense caused by the wider literacy is a more difficult question to answer.

There are six main components in this revolutionary advance. They were all in place before 500 B.C., but they cannot be detected before 600 B.C., (or outside the greek world at this time). The first is, in a word, logic. At its simplest this is the awareness of contradictions, along with the refusal to accept explanations, statements and so on, which can be shown to contain contradictions. Some logic was involved in the earliest greek mathematics, especially in geometrical theorems[3].

The second component may be called abstraction. Thinkers must learn to use words in an abstract sense, and not simply in relation to actual concrete situations. By this means words are understood to have general significance. In particular the thinker must not personalise the things under consideration, especially if they are inanimate objects. It is uncertain if this depersonalisation of the world had been satisfactorily achieved before level IV[4], but personalisation is normal in non-literate peoples; it seems to be a kind of legacy of the pan-animist, spirit/body idea of level I.

The third component is secularity. This is arguably the simplest, but ultimately perhaps the most far reaching component. As one historian of greek 'science' put it – "they left out the gods". The omission of spirits, gods and mythic beings from all attempts to understand and analyse the physical world is in fact a giant step forward, and the idea is not found in greek civilisation earlier than the end of the seventh century B.C., or in any parallel culture. This development leads to the concept that questions about the nature of the world are best dealt with by reason, and not by recourse to religion or myth. For those who have grown up in a rational tradition, it is hard to realise how revolutionary this advance is!

The next component is the search for natural order. In some ways this was foreshadowed in the preceding culture levels by the idea of 'divine order', but natural order or even nature is a new idea. Once we have left out the gods, we have to search for some other kind of order. In fact the greeks seem to have invented the idea of nature, and they used the word 'phusis' for it. Perhaps the most significant advance here was the concept that we should be searching for generalisations or 'laws', and expecting to find them.

The fifth component is the abstract idea of theory or hypotheses (both greek words). This is a new concept, inviting the creation of generalisations or solutions to problems of various kinds, but recognising that these are candidate solutions, rather than known or certain answers. Where the problem is not easy to solve, it helps to have different people coming up with different conjectural solutions, to improve our chances of getting a good answer; and it helps to have a tolerant or pluralist attitude towards such attempts.

The last component is the use of reasoned critical discussion (not on emotional or moral grounds, but on factual grounds). In particular this involves using logic to deduce from theories what their consequences would be, if they were in fact true. These consequences can then be evaluated in the light of known fact. Other forms of scrutiny can also be used, such as looking for inconsistencies[5].

Although the concept of rationality is notoriously difficult to define, these six components offer a good approximation. The absence of all six would definitely indicate the absence of rationality, and the presence of all six would be a good guide to its presence. In greco-roman and medieval civilisation, evidence of rationality is widespread, but in each case it tends to be a preliminary and incomplete version of rationality.

The idea that we can start from a hypothesis or conjecture, deduce logically from it a set of consequences, and then see if these coincide with the known facts, is often called hypothetico-deductivism. When we come to examine the question of whether the thought level of the hellenic greeks is analogous in some way to any of Piaget's stages of thought or cognitive development, the answer is obvious. No detailed analysis of the thought of level IV is needed in this case. Hypothetico-deductivism is the central definition of Piaget's stage IV thought - the formal operational stage. In the earlier culture levels we have examined in previous chapters, hypothetico-deductivism is apparently totally absent. But in the greek world, from the sixth century B.C. onwards, it is definitely present, and is distinctive of at least a part of the educated classes. This greek tradition of rationality survives down to medieval times and into the scientific revolution dealt with in the next chapter.

It is worth a brief digression at this point to examine the apparent facts surrounding the origin of rationality as we have characterised it above. The 'philosopher' Thales (circa 624-545 B.C.) is traditionally credited with being the first person (greek or otherwise) to speculate on questions of 'science', mathematics and philosophy. His pupil was Anaximander (circa 610-540 B.C.), who in turn was supposed to have taught Anaximenes. All these 'philosopher-scientists' lived in the city-state of Miletus (in Ionia on the aegean coast of present day western Turkey, south of Ephesus). Thus strictly this school was 'asiatic'. Pythagoras (circa 570-500) was also said to have been a pupil of Anaximander. He came from the island of Samos, near Ephesus, before transferring to Croton in southern Italy. The next two 'philosophers' also came from the Ionian region, and then the focus shifted to southern Italy and Sicily. All this reminds us that the greek world was one of very widespread and independent city states, and mainland Greece was not the original focus of philosophy. This focus was firstly Ionia in Asia minor, and secondly southern Italy and Sicily ('Magna Graecia'). The kind of pioneer rationality of Thales and his successors subsequently spread over much of Europe and the near east, but it seems that the tradition originated in just one place – Ionia.

Thales is personally credited with producing several geometrical theorems, which involve the use of logic, and there is little doubt that at least elementary logic is involved in the work of the first four philosophers, not to mention their successors. (It was Aristotle, two hundred years later, who first formalised logic and the use of syllogisms). The other components of rationality also appeared early. The early greek philosophers undoubtedly used abstract concepts. It is clear that they discussed questions of pioneer 'science' without invoking gods or other mythic figures; and thus the component of secularity is present at this time. Equally it is evident that the early philosophers (who are recorded as searching for the 'first principle' of the cosmos) were engaged in a quest for natural order or generalisations. They clearly formulated theories or hypotheses, and we find them submitting each others theories to critical scrutiny.

It is significant that the first four philosophers all offered different (or competing) theories on the question of the basic underlying nature of their world. There is no hint that Thales objected to Anaximander's view, nor that either of them tried to expel their successors from the 'Milesian' school. All the evidence suggests that they expected and encouraged competing views, and the idea that the rigid authority of the founder had to be accepted on pain of expulsion is quite absent. In due course, the philosophers were quite critical, even insulting, about each other's views, and this is roughly how rational enquiry proceeds to this day.

By far the simplest explanation of the scanty reports we have of the first philosophers is that the tradition of rational and critical research began with Thales and the Milesian school around the middle of the sixth century B.C.; and that is why I have referred to this intellectual revolution as the 'Thalean revolution', and more importantly to the continuing tradition of rationality as the Thalean tradition. There are good reasons to think that this tradition continued not just through the hellenic and hellenistic periods, until it was incorporated in the roman world, but also through the so-called dark ages, until we begin to find serious new work from medieval philosophers like Siger of Brabant, Roger Bacon and William of Occam[6]. The continuity of the tradition of interest in such matters is to some extent underlined by the fact that, even in the depths of the 'dark ages', thinkers like Plato and Aristotle were taken more seriously than they were in the roman period.

Changes in religion

What happens to 'religion' and myth during the fourth level of human culture? First we need to stress that these do not simply die, as soon as a slender tradition of rationality emerges. Religion survives, as it survives today, because it fills a need. While often it continues in a more or less pure form, as does rationality, what is characteristically new in this level is a kind or fusion or coexistence of the two, which I have called ratio-mythic duality.

We may look at just a few examples of this duality. We find that the school of Pythagoras pursues 'philosophy' of considerable merit, while also being a religious sect, derived from the orphics and the cult of Dionysus. Then again Plato deliberately uses myth in his dialogues as a technique of persuasion. Euhemerus of Sicily offered around 300 B.C. an analysis which combined traditional myth with rational arguments. It has been an influential book, and has given us the word euhemerism for this kind of rationalisation of myth. The 'scholastic' philosophers of medieval Europe, notably figures like St. Thomas Aquinas and Abelard, combine strict rationality with traditional religion. St. Anselm uses ingenious rational arguments to try to demonstrate the existence of a deity.

A very marked feature of religion in level IV is the decline of polytheism, the invocation and worship of a multiplicity of gods. In the preceding level III, polytheism was near universal[7]. If we examine the three 'units' of level IV, greek, roman and medieval, we find that in the first, polytheism is in a sense the 'official' religion, (though not obviously state-promoting,) but it was already in decline. In the roman phase, polytheism is soon in decline; (in the late roman and byzantine empires, it is no longer the state religion and is becoming rare.) In the high period of medieval Europe, polytheism is effectively dead.

The same span of time sees the rise of monotheism, (along with ratio-mythic duality). As early as about 500 B.C., the philosopher Xenophanes is talking about the 'one' god. Judaism, at least by the fourth century B.C., is a monotheistic religion, and many non-jews in the hellenistic world were apparently converted to monotheism. Christianity begins to be the 'normal' religion over a wide area in the centuries after Christ, and it is joined by Islam. By around 800 to 1000 A.D., in those areas which were genuinely at level IV, monotheism is the dominant form of religion. (Ideas of the second sub-level will be treated in part two, below.)

Section ii   **Economy and Technology**

The most far-reaching economic change in level IV is the introduction of coinage. It is generally thought that circular metal coins were first introduced in the state of Lydia, just inland in western Turkey from Ionia. Lydia was not a greek state, but it was influenced by greek culture; (indeed it is claimed that Thales himself acted as advisor to the king, Croesus). Be that as it may, coinage spreads very quickly, after its introduction about 625 B.C., across the greek world, and it was from here primarily, and from the persian empire, that it passed to a wide variety of later cultures[8].

The importance of coinage lies in the effect that it had on the ease of trade and commerce. So great was its impact that there was something like an explosion in trading. Previously any kind of transaction involved barter, or at best objects of accepted value (iron currency bars, small weights of precious metals etc.). The greek world also had the advantage that it extended from the Black Sea and the Nile to the western mediterranean. Thus long distance trading was relatively easy by sea, using efficient shipping, which they were developing at the time. The effects of this increased trade include greater total wealth (and *per capita* wealth). Merchants and traders, who tended to rank rather low in level III, now acquire a higher status.

Ironworking was extremely rare before 1000 B.C. The smelting of iron seems to have been invented by the Hittites, an archaic state in central Turkey. They are thought to have kept it a deliberate secret until the fall of the Hittite state after 1200 B.C. Then it spreads into other parts of western Asia, and then to the greek world[9].

There are no obvious major advances in agriculture in greco-roman times, but iron tools must have helped improve preparation of the soil, compared to most level III societies. Where we have provisional estimates, they indicate an increase in the population density of perhaps fifty percent on average. Similarly the scanty data from demography indicate a small reduction in average premature mortality, and probably a small increase in average life expectancy[10]. Medicine, as we now understand the term, begins in level IV, with Hippocrates (floruit circa 500 B.C.) and his school. This is the first mainly rational attempt to deal with health problems, as opposed to the largely mythic approach of previous levels.

The great innovation in building during level IV was the arch, constructed with wedge-shaped key stones. Not long afterwards the related concept of the vaulted roof was put into practice. The arch was apparently developed in southern Italy by about 200 B.C., (at about the time the romans were incorporating this area). Exactly which culture invented the arch is unclear, but the introduction of concrete shortly afterwards is a roman achievement. Archaic states of level III already had simple machines, but in the new level they were improved a little. Presses for olives and grapes were developed. Archimedes invented his remarkable 'screw' for lifting water, and other ingenious devices as well.

Section iii Political and Social Organisation

In archaic literate states, autocratic rule was nearly universal[11]. When we come to level IV, the situation is different. Before 550 B.C. the greek city states had mainly rid themselves of dynastic monarchies of the autocratic kind. These had faded so far into the past that the name 'Basileus' (king) had come to mean a religious official. Similarly the romans had abandoned kingship before their period of expansion and prominence.

A completely new kind of government is tried in level IV, and it has given us both the concept and the name of democracy. In this system all the male citizens are entitled to attend assembly meetings, at which policy is decided by voting, and officials are appointed. There are different versions of assembly democracy, but a favourite idea is that magistrates and other officials should be chosen by lot. (It is thus significantly different from any recent western model of democracy.) The idea emerged only slowly, and for much of hellenic greek history, democracy alternates with 'tyranny'[12] or 'oligarchy'. In the roman period, the republic is a kind of democracy, having the senate and various kinds of 'curia' or 'comitia'[13]. (With the establishment of the roman empire, only traces of democracy survive – the senate and 'tribunes' for example.) In spite of all these variations, there is a continuing ethos, throughout early level IV (i.e. the Alpha-Novaric), which holds that absolute or autocratic rule should be avoided. In later level IV, the situation is significantly different, and it will be discussed in part two.

Slavery remains common throughout the earlier part of level IV; and there is a lower class of peasants, labourers and craftsmen. Above this, in the greek world, is only a class of richer citizens, along with a rather poorly defined 'aristocracy'. Thus we can generally find only three of four classes, compared to the previous level which had more social classes, and these were more rigidly separated. Compared to the archaic states, level IV had little trace of polygamy. The taking of several wives, which had been routine in the upper classes of level III society, was of course effectively banned by christianity (in later level IV). What is rather surprising is that polygamy seems already to have been absent from the start of level IV.

In the period leading up to hellenic civilisation, a number of law codes were formulated in various city states. Thereafter a system of law courts and justice was elaborated, which had the unusual feature that each citizen was allowed to, and expected to, conduct his own case for prosecution or in defense. Because many, particularly the less well off, had difficulty with this, some educated people – the sophists (maligned by Plato and his coterie) – would coach the citizen for a fee. The three skills they concentrated on were grammar, rhetoric and logic. The first would aid the presentation of the case in correct language, while the second and third would make the argument seem more cogent and rational. This course became known as the trivium, and along with four subjects called the quadrivium[14], was basic to university education in medieval Europe. It seems probable that the emphasis placed on logic gave a particular 'stamp' to greek (and level IV) thought, and this to some extent explains their prowess in the rational evaluation of ideas, which was new to this level.

Part Two   Later level IV (the Beta-Novaric)

The second sub-level of level IV begins somewhere between 700 and 1000 A.D., and ends about 1500 A.D.

Section i   **Technology and Economy**

Two advances in technology are of sufficient long term importance to serve as the definition of this new sub-level. The first concerns the plough. Previously ploughs had been of the scratch variety, in which a vertical blade makes a cut in the soil and creates a modest furrow. Sometime between 600 and 900 A.D. a far more effective plough is introduced in Europe. For a start it has wheels, and is easier to move over the ground, ploughing to a consistent depth. The first cutting element is an iron knife or 'coulter' which cleaves the soil. Behind this is a metal shoe and a twisted 'mould board', which get under the turf; because of the curve, they turn the whole top soil over. Especially for the heavy soils of Europe (but latterly in other regions as well) this is a superior aid to soil preparation, particularly if pulled by oxen or shire horses[15]. Along with other advances this significantly increases food yields; and like the next innovation it has important social consequences.

The second invention, made at about the same time, is deceptively simple. It is the iron stirrup[15]. [Earlier forms of stirrup had been used in various parts of Asia. Loops of rope tend to be uncomfortable and easily cut in combat. One of the earliest forms of metal stirrup had only room for a toe hold – so needed bare feet!] The european iron stirrup (with other equestrian refinements) makes riding easier and more secure. It is often used with heavy 'shire horses', and its first importance is military. Previously horsemen were used in war, but they could not charge or lance at their enemies; it was almost impossible to avoid being dismounted. With the combination of the metal stirrup, a powerful horse, and armour, mounted shock combat becomes a potent force in war. The 'knight' is born, and becomes a key figure in medieval battles.

The small scale use of iron for making tough tools goes back, as we noted, to a few advanced level III states, and is normal in level IV. But it seems that there were two big advances over the relatively modest use of ironwork found up to the end of the greco-roman period. The second is in the industrial revolution; but the first, less well known and poorly documented, falls in this sub-level, and occurred somewhere around 800-1100 A.D., primarily in the more northerly parts of Europe. According to

Lynn White, iron is now mined and worked on a much larger scale than previously; and it became less expensive[15].

One more example of the generally improved technology of this time may be offered. It is mill-power. Hitherto power for machines had only been available from human muscle, and less often, animal strength. Now with mill-power it can be derived from wind and water. There is scanty evidence that water-powered mills already existed in the roman empire, but were very rare. Between about 800 and 1200 A.D. both wind and water mills become common. They are used for tasks like grinding flour, and early forms of belt and gear wheel drive become typical.

Evidently the second sub-level of the level IV (the Beta-Novaric) saw much more advance in technology than the first sub-level. Scholars have speculated in the past that this might have been because the first sub-level (Alpha-Novaric) involved a society with plenty of slaves or conscripts to do the heavy work, and the greeks and romans put low priority on the development of labour saving devices, or aids to lighten heavy work. As we shall see in the next section, slavery, at least in a strict sense, disappeared in the second sub-level.

During the last century or so of level IV, an entirely new activity begins. This is the global exploration, which was spearheaded by voyagers sponsored by the iberian countries. They used ever improving ocean-going ships, with the square rigging more suitable for long voyages. A combination of skill and determination enables them to explore, and increasingly map, the coasts of continents like Africa and Asia, which were already known. They are also the first europeans, or indeed the the first people from any advanced civilisation, to discover 'new' continents – first the americas and then australasia and oceania. The motives were mixed and complex – adventure, trade with the 'indies', conversion of new christians and seizure of treasure.

Section ii **Political, Social and Military Organisation**

The social and political system of this later sub-level differs considerably from anything found in the earlier sub-level or previously. The states of this period normally have kings, but the kind of autocratic rule, typical of the level III archaic states, is no longer normal. Instead we have what is usually called the 'feudal' social order, typical of medieval western christendom. In this system there are several formal classes, from the royals and nobles at the top, down through other larger land owners (knights, 'squires' etc.), and smaller farmers (villeins etc.) to serfs.

One of the most important changes in this sub-level is the withering away of slavery in its strict sense. This seems to have become complete somewhere between the ninth and eleventh centuries. Slaves proper can by definition be bought and sold. But serfs, who effectively replace them as the lowest class, can not be bought and sold, though there would often be practical difficulties to prevent them leaving their employers. This development represents a dramatic change in society. We must remember that the christian church objected to christians being enslaved, so that increasingly the only possible slaves are from distant non-christian lands.

The four or so classes of feudal society differ in their wealth and status, but all are enmeshed in the feudal system. The serfs and villeins have feudal obligations of agricultural and military service to those above them. But more importantly the obligations run downwards as well. The farmer has to feed and protect his serfs, and the knights have to protect their tenants and farmers from attack or other misfortune. The feudal lord has to protect the local landowners and organise them militarily. The king is obligated to protect everyone. Failure to fulfil these obligations is not lightly tolerated in feudalism. A weak king or lord will, if necessary, be replaced.

There are other respects in which the political power of the monarch or his officials is limited. For a start the church has considerable powers, and can challenge the civil authorities in some areas. More importantly, the monarchy in this sub-level is obliged to try to work with various 'councils'. (To some extent this tradition goes back to tribal farmers, who regularly had a council of elders, and there may in the more northerly and westerly parts of Europe have been an uninterrupted continuity of this idea.) Examples of such councils are the saxon 'witenagemot', the french 'parlement' and the parliament of Simon de Montfort. The common people do not attend these councils, and have to rely on their local lords or knights to represent them. As these councils develop, they come to include other sectors of society, such as the church, the towns, the craft guilds and merchants. This kind of political organisation is markedly different from the greek 'democracy' of citizen assemblies. These new councils are prototypes of a 'representative' form of democracy, (which does not come to be elected by universal suffrage until the twentieth century).

Earlier we noted the significance of the invention of the iron stirrup, and the rise of heavily armed knights. These are a significant element in the social system we have been examining, but even more directly they revolutionise warfare, which is now dominated by knights in full armour, who are difficult to defeat in battle. Their importance even overshadows the first primitive firearms of the late medieval period. Lastly castles and advanced siegecaft are now highly significant in war.

We may end by noting some new features in myth and religion. First there is the rise of a cult of romantic love, associated with the troubadour movement, and romances like Tristan and Iseult, and the Arthurian legends. At the same time, a more abstract and intense spirituality is found in christianity. These phenomena are quite new.

Chapter SEVEN   THE LEVEL OF INDUSTRIAL CIVILISATION: Level V
(Industrial and Science-based Nation-States; the Cenoric from 1700 A.D. onwards[1])

This chapter will be relatively short. The period of three centuries is by far the shortest of all the levels, even though it is arguable that more change has occurred in this level than in any previous level. As far as the twentieth century (which makes up the second sub-level) is concerned, many readers will, like myself, have lived through more than half of it, and know all too well what it was like. By contrast, the earlier levels are widely misunderstood, and too often assumed to possess the same kind of characteristics (and mindset) as the current level of culture; this is why they have been given more detailed scrutiny in this book.

Section i   **Science, Technology and Economy**

The Scientific Revolution of the Proto-Cenoric [2]

The importance of the scientific revolution can perhaps best be explained briefly by saying that before 1500 A.D., the idea of systematic research in fields like physics and astronomy, using experiments and an empirical approach, would have been unknown. By 1700 A.D. this scientific approach, and the equipment like telescopes and microscopes to make it possible, are already well established, in a group of western european countries[3]. (Indeed the tradition of research was already so well established by this time, that it was unlikely to lapse.) The scientific revolution is the prelude to the industial era, because the industrial revolution followed directly on from it. Science was no doubt a major factor in its origin.

Copernicus is the principal pioneer of the scientific revolution[4]. His works (the *Commentariolus* of 1510, and the postumous *de Revolutionibus* of 1543) record the great advance he made in the understanding of the movements of the bodies in the solar system. After him many scientists are known to have made significant contributions to the emergence of science at this time. Galileo in particular was making an outstanding contribution to the birth of modern physics. But the culmination of this scientific revolution (which occurred within a decade or so of 1700 A.D.) can best be attributed to Isaac Newton (especially his work on universal gravitation of 1687 and optics of 1704). His discoveries had an enormous impact on contemporary thinking, and were quickly accepted by scientists across those countries which were participating in the scientific movement.

The Industrial Revolution and Level V

We can trace the dawn of the industial revolution to about 1700 A.D. The construction of the first coke-fired blast furnace in 1709, at the Shropshire locality of Coalbrookdale in the west midlands of England, is often regarded as the most appropriate event to mark the beginning of this revolution[5]. The industrial revolution is complete by about 1860. Its most important elements include industrial iron production, steam power, rail transport pulled by steam locomotives, and mechanised mass production. Shipbuilding shows spectacular advances. Throughout this time, coal is fundamental. The intermediate technology of the two previous levels is replaced by industrial and powered machine technology.

The industrial revolution leads directly, in the later nineteenth century, to the wide use of gas and electricity for power and lighting; and then to the use of petroleum or fuel oil, which makes practicable the internal combustion engine, subsequently the most convenient power for transport. In a parallel development, processes for the reliable manufacture of steel are developed by the 1860s, and steel mills provide large quantities of cheap steel for advanced industrial technology.

During the industrial revolution, mechanisation and scientific advances extend to agriculture. This agrarian revolution makes possible over a few centuries an increase in population greater than any that had previously occurred, since hunting gave way to farming. The increase is regularly over four or five times. In some of the more industrialised countries it is over ten times, and densities of over 200 persons per square kilometre are common in this level, while densities of over thirty persons per sq. km., for whole countries, were almost unknown in previous levels[6].

Technical advances of various kinds contribute greatly to this process. More sophisticated selection of crops allows significantly higher yields, and livestock is also much improved by selective breeding. Various methods of fertilising and pest control lead to much greater productivity. The heavy wheeled plough originating in the previous level had already held out the promise of much better soil preparation, but further improvements in equipment resulting from the industrial revolution, and in due course powered traction of farm machinery, brings new land under cultivation and ploughs existing land deeper. Some industrial countries at first relied on importing food, but in due course they are able to produce surpluses of food, and even to export them.

The best known advances in the agrarian revolution, such as the seed drill, mechanical reapers and combine harvesters, are most significant for reducing the amount of labour needed on the land. Often this caused temporary unemployment, but it encouraged labour to switch to industry. Increasingly the majority of the population work not in food production, but in the production of other goods in factories, and in various service 'industries'. From the situation in hunter-gatherer societies, where almost every able bodied adult worked on gaining subsistence, mankind has moved progressively to a situation in which only a few percent of the workforce are involved directly in food production. Cities, towns and industrial areas expand, along with the percentage of people living or working in them.

The fact that part of the increase in population in advanced industrial countries was made possible by food imports, underlines another major change. Global trade, using a new breed of faster ships, which could undertake longer voyages than before, expands much more rapidly in the last three hundred years than even before. It has an outstanding effect on the growth of wealth in modern states, and there are important consequences for the social make-up of the population. (The origins of these developments go back to the age of exploration mentioned in the previous chapter, which begins in or just before the fifteenth century, and accelerates during the scientific revolution with the first voyages round the world, and the exploration of Australasia and the Pacific.) Regular global transport is made possible by the larger and more powerful ships of level V, which in the nineteenth century are powered by steam. The railways revolutionised transport on land, (and even before them, canals were a useful form of transport for heavy loads.)

There had of course been some economic change in level IV, but it was much greater, and of more profound significance, in level V. Capital is available as never before. Much of the growth of industry is financed by 'venture capital', money loaned by banks or derived from the issue of stocks and shares. Waged labour is normal from the start of level V, and has almost replaced serfdom, as well as the 'payment-in-kind' of earlier levels of culture. There are intermittent taxes and tarifs of various kinds, but trade and commerce is more free and more profitable in level V than ever before. The economy of advanced western states grows more rapidly than previously, and new wealth is created faster. The *per capita* wealth of these countries grows to an unprecedented degree. With capitalism, there is truly an 'economic' revolution, alongside the industrial and other revolutions. Hitherto only the most elementary economic ideas had existed, but in the early part of the industrial era, a new theory and analysis of economics arises; it is especially the work of Adam Smith, Ricardo and Malthus.

Science, Technology and Economy in later level V (the Neo-Cenoric)

The level of 'industrial' culture has been rather arbitrarily subdivided into two sub-levels, with the boundary set close to 1900 A.D. Both the pace of change and the relentlessness of change during level V are of an entirely new order, but this is a very convenient place to situate a boundary. In science, advanced physical science begins between about 1896 and 1905 with the discovery of radioactivity (Bequérel), subatomic particles (Rutherford and Thompson), quantum theory (Planck) and relativity (Einstein). In biology, the placing of mendelian heredity and genetics on a sound scientific foundation happens just after 1900.

Between 1886 and 1900 fuel oil begins to replace coal as the most important source of power for land transport, with the development of the internal combustion engine. This new engine leads to the first powered personal transport or automobile (by Benz and Daimler), and the first powered passenger aircraft (Wright brothers). The technology which makes easy, and even global, communication possible dates from around or shortly before 1900 - telephone (Bell); radio (Marconi). Numerous other advances occurred at about this time, some of roughly equal importance. The pace of change in the most recent century of level V has been greater than in any previous century.

It is hardly necessary to point out that the development of science and technology has manifested a further acceleration since the 1930s, barely affected by the second world war. Nor is it of any objective interest that many people can not even consider the changes which have occurred in this area, without trying to categorise them as bad or good. Such an approach can never increase our factual knowledge, and will always be subject to dispute. With this in mind, we may mention just a few significant advances. The splitting of the atom led to nuclear technology. The development of the transistor improved the performance of radio and television. The jet engine and parallel improvements in aerospace technology made global air transport efficient, quick and eventually relatively cheap. Space rockets, radiotelescopes and artificial satellites have advanced both cosmology and communication.

A further era of acceleration can be detected from the 1970s onward. From the first primitive computers of the previous generation, the microchip made possible cheap and miniaturised computer technology of awesome power. The discovery of the role of DNA in the genetic make-up of life in 1953, led on in this new period to the first elementary knowledge of the genome, and finally a near complete reading of the human genome. In the field of economics, the increase in *per capita* wealth is most obvious in this period; and there is even something close to a consensus in economic theory, of how a prosperous low inflation economy can be assured.

Demographic Effects of Culture Level V

As we saw when discussing the agrarian revolution, the improved agriculture of level V provides far more food with far less labour. The population of individual advanced 'industrial' countries rises in some cases to more than ten times that of the preceding level, even if one does not count the many who went overseas to the americas, australasia and other areas of european influence. During the twentieth century however, population increase in the leading european level V states was in fact small by choice (birth control), and not by necessity; (immigrants have been the main cause of population increase in the advanced west.) Agricultural productivity has continued to rise during this period, diminishing the need for imported food, and causing the 'food mountains', as well as policies like 'set aside' to decrease production. People eat (and waste) more than in previous centuries, and obesity is an increasing problem.

The most spectacular demographic changes have been in the area of premature mortality and life expectancy[7]. Premature mortality (meaning here the average percentage of deaths under 16 years of age) was still high in the preceding level – probably rarely under 35 % in representative samples. During the eighteenth century in level V countries, the average seems to be in the bracket 25-45%; (if reliable figures were available on large samples, there would probably be a much smaller bracket mainly under 35%). In the nineteenth century, the bracket is down to the range 15-40%. Between 1900 and 1970 the bracket is in the order of 3 to 30%. Since 1970 the average percentage, on much improved data, is regularly below 4%. In spite of the large brackets and uncertainties involved, the decrease in infant and child mortality across a range of level V countries is undoubted and dramatic.

Life expectancy[7] in level IV was only about 25 years on average at birth, and by age 15 perhaps around 33-35 years. In the eighteenth century, level V experiences an increase in birth expectancy to about 30-33 years, and in adult expectancy to 50-55 years. In the nineteenth century this increases to about 38 (birth) and 58 years(adult).

The greatest increase is found in the twentieth century, during which birth expectancy passes from below 50 to over 75 years, while adult expectancy moves from perhaps about 60 to over 75 years.

The reader will note that whereas, until the twentieth century, life expectancy at birth is markedly lower than it is for those who have reached maturity, the two are quite close together by the end of the twentieth century in advanced level V societies. For pre-human and ape societies, the birth expectancy was nearer half the adult expectancy. An equally remarkable change is that in all levels before level V, male life expectancy was on average a few years longer than for females. But almost from the start of level V, the situation is reversed, and female expectancy consistently averages somewhat higher than it is for males. This is presumably due to more successful child birth practices used at this level.

The principal reason for the fall in premature mortality and increase in life expectancy involves improvements in medicine and health. Medical science has been remarkably successful in level V in eradicating killer epidemics like diphtheria and smallpox. Fatalities in childbirth are now rare. Similar improvements have helped to prolong life. Doctors are numerous in advanced level V societies, and the technology of life saving is sophisticated and expensive.

The impact of humans on their natural environment is far greater in level V. Agriculture, industrial use and management of land have a vastly increased effect on the landscape. The pressure on wildlife has been much greater, but this has been accompanied by a growing scientific expertise concerning nature, and massive programmes (like nature reserves, and national parks) designed to protect it. The resources lavished on protecting and saving wildlife are far greater than in any previous level.

Section ii **Political, Social and Military Organisation**

During level V, the nation-state is the ideal form of state, in the eyes of most people of this level. Before the fifteenth century, the idea hardly existed. There was a vague concept of ethnic groups with a common language or 'nations', mainly of tribal origin, and there was the idea of the state, but the two were not linked. Of course absolutely 'pure' nation-states (uniform ethnically, linguistically and culturally) have never existed. The abandonment of the state, furthermore, has never been achieved or even attempted.

Modern concepts of democracy go back to the beginning of level V. They are very different from the idea of the (citizen assembly) democracy of the greek city states, (which bequeathed little more than the word). Increasingly government has been in the hands of elected 'representatives', and not an absolute monarch or tyrant. At first only a small minority of adults had votes, but in late level V it has become normal for all adults to have a vote[8]. Political parties also became normal during level V.

In the two preceding levels, social organisation was to some extent fixed or rigid. In level V it has become increasingly fluid and pluralistic. Any certainties or universals concerning class, which may have existed before 1700, have probably all disappeared during the current level. Whereas in the preceding period, only a tiny percentage of the population could be classified as 'upper or middle' class, and the vast majority were evidently 'poor' or 'lower class', in level V the balance shifts. In the last half century or so, an overtly lower class has ceased to be the majority. (Recent polls in Britain for example revealed that the majority of the population do not class themselves as lower class.)

In the same period, everyone who does not have an adequate income to survive on has been allowed to receive from the state some form of welfare assistance or payments. Many of the richest and most influential people of this same half century have come from humble backgrounds. Hereditary classes, which received preferment in past centuries and past levels, no longer do in late level V. Kinship has declined in importance across society in general. Often only close kin remain in touch and extended kin do not, in spite of much easier communications.

The family remains the most basic social unit for most of the industrial era, but once again the last half century has seen a trend against it. Marriage breakdown has evidently become much commoner in most level V states. This, and comparable forms of diminution of the family, are most apparent in what on many criteria are among the most advanced states. Other signs of family breakdown are the frequency of cohabitation with no intention of marriage, and the frequency of illegitimate fatherless children. (According to one theory, an 'underclass', characterised by illegitimacy, welfare dependency, high crime and vandalism, is rapidly increasing.) More generally late level V is characterised in social and other spheres by a pluralism or bewildering variety of forms of behaviour, and an unprecedentedly rapid arrival and decline of new forms of behaviour.

In the field of politics, a number of conflicting objectives have been pursued or advocated. Some of the more important polarities are:-

Democracy versus Totalitarianism

Individual liberalism versus Collectivism

Market liberalism versus Economic socialism (state ownership and dirigism)

Individual responsibility versus Statutory universal welfarism

Strict approach to crime prevention versus Tolerant attitude to crime

Political 'correctness' versus Freedom of opinion

It is obvious that warfare in the industrial era has been quite different from any hostilities before 1500 A.D. Between about 1700 and 1860 A.D. firearms (with the development of the rifle, revolver and breech loading guns) come to have a decisive effect on war. (They had existed from about 1400 A.D. in a very primitive form – allegedly of limited use beyond frightening cavalry horses.) By the 1860s a force without firearms would have stood no chance against a similar sized force with up-to-date firearms. Twentieth century innovations are numerous; fighter aircraft, submarines, tanks, aircraft carriers and early warning systems like radar, are just a few. The 'high-tec' innovations of recent decades have moved war to a new level of sophistication, and partly for this reason, war between advanced industrial states has been avoided. The main level V states of Europe have not had a local war for over half a century. (Small wars in countries peripheral to the advanced level V states have meanwhile been common.) For the major level V states, violence in civil society has been much more of a problem.

Section iii Communication and Thought

The industrial level is one of continuous revolution in communication. The 'modern' method of printing, using moveable metal type, was invented just before the scientific revolution. The impact of this was slow at first; but, by the time of the industrial revolution, printed books are beginning to become inexpensive and commonplace. A regular coach mail service becomes available from early in level V, and a true postal service using stamps, and offering delivery to any address, is introduced in the first half of the nineteenth century. Newspapers are already common in the same century.

By the second half of the nineteenth century, the telephone and the telegraph have been developed, along with the typewiter. Radio is operative by the start of the twentieth century, and could increasingly broadcast globally. There is even more remarkable progress during the remainder of this century. Cinema and film become common in the first half of the century, and are joined by television. The latter becomes almost universal in the second half of the century in level V societies, soon to be available in high quality colour and with pictures instantly from around the globe. Recorded sound improves and becomes cheaper through the century, to be joined by the significant advance of video tape, which soon also becomes cheap. Recently 'fax' and e-mail have been joined by the internet, in a rapidly growing world wide 'web' of communication. Satellites have also had a revolutionary impact on long distance communication, and techniques of navigation and geographical positioning.

In the prehistoric levels, I and II, mankind had the spoken word only. In levels III and IV there was both the spoken and the written word. At the end of level IV, the printed word was added. By late level V, we have the typed word, the recorded word, the broadcast word and the word on computer and internet screens. The word had come a long way.

It is debatable whether thought is any more 'advanced' in level V than before. The 'hardware' brain has obviously not changed much or at all. The 'software' consists of a veritable mountain of information, along with a mode of thinking which, at its most advanced, includes both the rational and the hypothetico-deductive form, developed in the previous level, as well as the newly developed (empirical and systematic) scientific thought. [Whether this amounts to a higher level of thinking than Piaget's stage IV formal operations is likely to be a matter of opinion.] Thus it is the build up of the 'software' – in books, records, encyclopaedias, data banks and so on – which is the main change. Only some of this new 'knowledge' is accurate, but the chances of identifying and correcting errors are greater than ever before.

In its modern sense, 'philosophy' no longer includes science and mathematics, or even politics and morality. That leaves things like logic, epistemology, meaning and other more or less abstract fields of thought[9]. Above all modern philosophy is obsessed with its own 'history', from the greeks onwards. Modern philosophy is usually taken to begin with pioneers like Descartes and Locke, and thus it coincides more or less with the start of level V.

Religion

In the preceding level, religion found itself co-habiting with pioneer rationality, philosophy, and a small 'secular' sector. However in level V, the secular sector grows vastly larger, and whole areas of activity like astronomy, law and especially the physical and biological sciences pursue their enquiries, less and less affected by myth and religious thought. Charles Darwin was by no means alone in the early nineteenth century, when he pursued biological investigations objectively, and with little reference to the biblical tradition in which he had grown up.

Nietsche may be dead, but religion in level V is definitely not dead. Generalising about religion in this level is made difficult by the fact that it is more varied and pluralistic than ever before. But this pluralism is itself new. Those intellectuals who continue to practise religion in late level V are much more likely to hold the view that religion and science (or factual truth) are separate phenomena, not in competition, but having different objectives and functions[10].

All states of level V were nominally christian until the twentieth century. Most remain predominantly christian[11], but this leads to uniformity only in a very limited way. The number of new 'religions' and sects, within and outside christianity, has increased dramatically. There has been a strong 'new age' movement, which has adopted and up-dated pre-christian ideas, like the earth mother, druids and even hunter-gatherer ideas like shamanism[12]. The industrial era seems to be unique in re-cycling religious or mythic ideas, drawn from considerably earlier levels, and this resuscitating of ideas like the earth mother and shamanism makes it seem superficially like earlier levels.

Morals

Previously 'morals' were a matter of custom, and then law. In level IV, philosophers like Plato and Aristotle began to treat morals or ethics as a subject for academic debate. This trend has continued in the industrial era, with the rise of 'moral philosophy' and related academic subjects. Religion has often been seen as inherently concerned with moral questions, and politicians have not been slow to enter this arena either. Unanimity on the answers to the moral problems has rarely been achieved. In late level V, morals have become a 'moral maze', as conflicting views and interests have proved irreconcilable. The fact is that society and its life have become immensely more complicated, and simple solutions that will please everyone are not possible.

Two examples of 'moral' change in the industrial era may be considered. Slavery was both normal and accepted in level III and sub-level IVa (and it survived into the twentieth century in societies which had not reached level V). In sub-level IVb (the

Beta-Novaric or medieval era), slavery became unacceptable, as we have seen, especially if it involved 'compatriots' (other europeans or christians) being enslaved. During the first half of the industrial era, there was a successful movement to make all forms of slavery and slave trading, including alien slavery, illegal[13]. This was soon adopted by all advanced countries, and it was sometimes enforced in remote areas of the world by europeans. This total ban on any kind of slavery was new in level V; but it was also an example of the new idea that 'westerners' should impose their moral convictions on others wherever they went.

As recently as the nineteenth century, it had been accepted with little demur, that states and tribes who had the necessary military muscle were justified in conquering their neighbours, and absorbing them into imperial rule. The idea that this was 'wrong' came only slowly. First it became the majority view that it was wrong to conquer other advanced states; and in due course this principle was extended globally. Empires in the past had sometimes lost their provinces through rebellion, but the voluntary conferring on them of statehood and self rule was quite exceptional. The 'granting' of dominion status to Canada, Australia and New Zealand around 1900 was something quite new in level V, without precedent in any previous level, and represented perhaps the most remarkable change in political and moral thinking ever. To a considerable extent, the two world wars of the twentieth century were fought over this crucial issue of whether peoples had a right to be free of foreign rule.

The 'Extra' Sector (iv) Leisure, Games and Aesthetics

In this sector, the significant contrasts are to do with games or sports with rules, formalised leisure activities, and a conscious concern for aesthetics. In the pre-literate levels (0, I and II), there was no trace of any of these. In the first two literate levels (III and IV) we do begin to find a trace of these, but it is very slight in level III. It is not much more obvious in level IV, but we need to mention some notable exceptions. The athletic 'games' of greek origin have been very influential, and prototypes of many modern games or sports can be detected in level IV. We should note before moving on to the vastly different situation of level V that the games of the greeks, like their theatre, began as a largely religious institution.

During level V, games and sport, along with organised leisure activities, have grown in a way previously unparalleled. Of course not everyone is involved in sports and games, but the millions who are, as spectators or participants, make this phenomenon of a quite different order. New games have been formalised to a much higher degree

than in previous levels. Other leisure activities have witnessed a similar explosion.
This affects not just what people spend their time on, or take most seriously in life. It
is also a massive section of the late level V economy.

Similarly the area of arts and entertainment has become a much more serious
concern than in any previous level. It is more important economically, becoming a
major source of wealth. A small industry has grown up around the business of
evaluation and criticism of art, music, film, theatre and similar arts.

A single, but important, example of change in the arts is in the field of music. The
greeks early in level IV discovered the underlying mathematical nature of music; this
was principally achieved by the pythagorean school. The notation of music was first
effectively formulated early in the second sub-level of level IV. But the music of
level V represented an even more spectacular advance. Sometime between 1400 and
1700 A.D., the combination of harmony and counterpoint began to bear fruit, and led
to polyphony. By the time of Bach and Handel at the dawn of level V, a much richer
form of music had been born.

To conclude, it is scarcely an exaggeration to say that this 'extra sector' dominates
most peoples lives, in a way which would have been inconceivable in any previous
level.

Chapter EIGHT   CONCLUSIONS: Interconnections, Directionality and Science

Interconnections of features within each level,

What reason could there be for each level of culture to exhibit the wide array of distinctive features that we have seen to be common to all (or most) of the societies which belong to the level in question? A plausible answer lies in the fact that these features are interconnected in various ways. They naturally go together.

Level I

Let us look at some of these networks of interconnections, starting with hunter gatherers, and routine meateating and huntcraft. There is little point in hunting meat-bearing animals, if they are not going to be eaten; (it was definitely not done for pure sport). In level I – before the breeding of meat-bearing animals or the advent of supermarkets – the obvious source for the high energy meat diet is hunting. (We have noted that scavenging would not provide regular meat nor large quantities.) Thus a diet in which meat is an important component requires regular hunting, at this level; and regular hunting only makes sense if it leads to a regular supply of meat for the diet. The two are clearly linked, in this situation, as part of a positive feedback.

Regular hunting and butchering of game animals would have been feasible for early humans, only if they had possessed some sort of tools, notably for cutting up the carcases, and for disabling the game. Before the beginning of hunting and meateating, there is no obvious advantage in early humans making tools. In other words there is a basic triple linkage of huntcraft, routine meateating and toolcraft. Huntcraft-meateating is in a positive feedback with simple toolcraft. The more suitable tools available, the better the hunting becomes; and the more hunting is pursued, the greater is the need for tools.

Several other features follow from this primary 'triple axis'. The realities of hunting and gathering the food supply require a nomadic or non-sedentary way of life, until in some way the food supply is sufficiently 'controlled' to allow them to settle (at which point they have moved beyond level I by definition). A nomadic way of life precludes permanent 'houses' and requires, as an alternative, temporary (or portable) shelters.

The absence of agriculture, or food production, allows only a low density of population (rarely more than 0.1 persons per square kilometre, over large areas) in hunter-gatherers. Because of this, their impact on the environment is usually modest.

Compared to their ape-like predecessors, early humans' meat diet provided the necessary energy and tissue replacement from a much smaller bulk of food. Less time was spent eating and, between hunts, there was more leisure than herbivores have. This free time facilitated the rise of 'culture', such as for example making up and reciting myths.

The extended dependency period in childhood of hunter-gatherers (and later levels) seems to be a fact. The 'specialisation' by sex of the male hunter role and the female gatherer and child-rearer role leads to the male-female bond, formalised in marriage. The need for juveniles to be cared for over a much longer period means that the family is a necessary unit at this level. The family leads to kinship concerns, and ideas such as incest.

Another train of linkages can be found in the thought of hunter-gatherers. A variety of observations that they regularly made (notably dreaming, the breath of life, the invisible but powerful wind, and 'expiration' at death) might be expected to suggest the idea of spirit, and thus the dualism of spirit and body. Once the idea that the spirit was the all-important component existed, this would focus their activities on attempts to alter circumstances by 'cajoling' the relevant spirits, and this is effectively the root of shamanism. The idea of metamorphosis is a central element of both shamanism, and the 'sacred bond' with their world, that hunters feel. Much of this type of thinking is further found to be closely similar to the type of thought found in children who have just acquired speech.

Level II

The primary linkage in the next level runs from the farming way of life to the necessity of sedentary living and thus permanent homes, and to the modest accumulation of property and 'wealth'. A second arm of this linkage is concerned with the diversification of material culture. Equipment for farming is much more varied, often including ceramic vessels (or a substitute for them). But there are a number of new technologies, like textiles or building. This leads to incipient craft specialisation, and a small but growing number of workers not involved directly in food production. The greatly increased population (which is made possible, and in a sense caused, by farming) also leads to a more complex society, of which craft specialisation is only one obvious example. Some leadership is necessary, and elementary 'political' power emerges. All these features are connected by a feedback process.

A complicated series of factors leads to the demise of egalitarianism, and the rise of social differentiation and of hierarchy. Level II is in this sense a level of change. The rise of leaders and the death of egalitarianism are reflected in their religious ideas – notably emergent gods and divine power. The changes in mythic thought mirror the change from the sub-stage of preconceptual thought found in child development, to the sub-stage of 'intuitive' thought, in which 'powers' replace 'will' (or spirit) as primary explanations. A simple ordered view of the world slowly replaces an 'unstructured' view. Complexity, and other 'points of view' begin to be appreciated.

Level III

The governing of a complex state necessitates recording things in writing; once both are in place, they tend to reinforce each other. Central authority makes possible very large scale projects like irrigation and flood defence. These have the effect of allowing (or even encouraging) moderately high population density. There is a downside to rigid centralised autocratic rule. Such closed societies, for reasons which are not always clear, are more prone to collapse. A pluralistic or open society has a variety of private ventures under way, and if some go wrong, others will probably succeed. A state with an autocratic monarch (who may be enlightened, or may be cruel and foolish) has, as it were, all its eggs in one basket, and is usually little diversified economically. This sort of situation seems to result in level III states collapsing within half a millennium or so.

The simple rites of pre-literate peoples are joined or replaced in this level by massive ceremonies, attended by thousands. That these have to be celebrated on the correct day (say midsummer) is a normal requirement, and this encourages the skill of calendar construction and astronomy of high accuracy. A new emphasis on astrology also requires good knowledge of planetary movements. The link may seem weak, but apparently all literate states felt these activities to be essential. They regularly resulted in the first accumulation of the kind of objective knowledge which led to science.

Level IV

The vowelled phonetic alphabet apparently encouraged a much higher level of literacy than ever before, and consequently resulted in a literate citizenry, and thus indirectly the concept of free citizens. That high literacy, and the invention and spread of rationality are linked together in a 'positive feedback' seems very likely. Once a tradition of rationality has been established, it is quite resistant to being stifled.

(Evidently rational hypothetico-deductivism 'overlaid' the existing sequence of thought development, and came to be incorporated in the thought of the more 'educated' young people from this time onwards.)

The intervention of coinage in an already established system of trading arrangements led to something like an explosion of trade and a great increase in wealth. This gave an upper tier of the population the leisure to indulge in 'philosophical' pursuits, which reinforced the new tradition of rationality.

Level V

The scientific revolution, along with a social and economic revolution, were the principle factors in allowing or causing the new industrial revolution. Once this new revolution was under way, there was a continuous feedback between it and the mature scientific tradition which emerged from the scientific revolution. Also the agrarian revolution was a by-product of this interaction. Industrial and agricultural enterprises required and financed the search for new scientific knowledge. The new scientific advances led to greater profits, and more reinvestment in industrial technology and scientific research. There was a similar feedback between the new capital-based economic system and the ongoing industrial revolution.

Another link can be traced between the rise of industry and wealth on the one hand, and the rise of a political system (representative democracy) which prevented centralised autocracy and tight state control. The kind of entrepreneurship which made the industrial era viable was only possible in the relative freedom provided by representative democracy. Similarly, economic theory only became possible when there was an opportunity to observe the economy being transformed, and to discuss it openly and without fear of repression.

Directionality

As we noted in the first chapter, there are a number of areas of culture in which features exhibit a clear direction of change through the five levels. The first is **population density** (and the related 'supporting capacity')[1].

From hunter-gatherers to tribal farmers the increase in population density is about one hundred times. From tribal farmers to literate states, the increase is in the order of two to four times. The increase from archaic states to greco-roman and medieval peoples is smaller, but still in the order of fifty percent. From this level IV to the late industrial era, an average of several representative countries shows an increase of over five times, and closer to ten times. During the twentieth century since 1920, population density in advanced level V countries has risen little[1], (except as a result of immigration and high immigrant birth rate). The carrying capacity from food production has undoubtedly risen several times during this period (1920-2000) and without policies like set-aside would have risen more. In no case as one passes across the levels has a whole level shown a decrease in population density, but there is clear evidence of increase in both population numbers and density.

Premature Mortality

For hunter-gatherers and pre-humans, deaths before sixteen years of age make up well over half of all deaths, while for tribal farmers the figure is close to fifty percent. In levels III and IV it seems likely to be in the range from one third to one half (when samples are large enough). In the industrial era, the proportion begins over or near a quarter, but in the twentieth century it falls to less than four percent in all the more advanced level V countries.

Life expectancy

Life expectancy at birth was low in the early levels (0, I and II) – no more than twenty to twenty-five years; it was medium low in levels III and IV – perhaps in the range twenty-two to thirty years; but it was markedly higher in level V – increasing from about thirty to over seventy years on average.

Wealth

In hunter-gatherer societies (and in apes), there was as we have seen no wealth or surpluses. Among tribal farmers, we find for the first time small surpluses, and a modest accumulation of goods. In early states there is a large accumulation of state wealth and surpluses, as well as modest wealth for many in the population, so that the average *per capita* ownership is almost certainly higher than in the previous level. The considerable boost in trade which came with coinage in level IV meant that there was almost certainly an overall increase in wealth, and it was spread over a wide range of the citizens. *Per capita* wealth in the late industrial level is indicated for example by figures for gross national product[2], which allows comparison of advanced level V countries with countries still close to the tribal farming level. They are several hundred times better off on this kind of measure.

Proportion of population involved in food 'production'

Here we are concerned with the percentage of the able adult population who are engaged in the direct production or acquisition of food. It is usually the inverse of the percentage primarily involved in jobs other than food production. For level I, somewhere in the order of ninety-nine percent of the able adults are primarily engaged in the acquisition of food. In level II the figure is still probably over ninety percent, as craft specialisation is rare among simple tribal farmers.

By contrast in late level V, the figure falls below ten percent to only a few percent. Reliable figures for levels III and IV are not available, but there is little doubt that they are between ninety and forty percent, and a little lower in level IV. Early in level V, rural population begins to fall below the urban population, and thus those involved primarily in food production would be well under fifty percent, and falling fast.

Numeracy

Apes do not have any number words. We have seen that numeracy was simple at the hunter-gatherer level. Various kinds of count based on two were the most advanced number system used, and counting beyond ten in number words was rare. In tribal farmers, systems of counting using either 5 and 10, or 5 and 20, as bases were normal, and it was common to be able to count over twenty or even over a hundred. In the first literate states, written numerals were introduced alongside number words, and counting into thousands was normal among those involved in tasks which required numbers or lists of commodities etc.. With the first 'philosophers'of level IV mathematics became more abstract, geometry was formalised, and a theoretical understanding of maths was widespread. Counting to high figures was easily accomplished. Level V, even as early as Newton, was capable of extremely sophisticated mathematics, and those skills have grown and become more widely used during this level than ever before. Numbers as high as billions and higher are routinely used.

Sources of power

Only muscle power, and some very simple devices were available to hunter-gatherers. This does not change very much with tribal farmers, but they occasionally used draught animals. Use of animal power was commoner in early states, and simple machines were used. In level IV they used machines, and horses were much commoner. In the second sub-level of level IV, wind and water mills became normal. The industrial era sees a completely new level of power use. It is the 'high energy' era, using coal on a large scale, and later gas, electricity, fuel oil and nuclear power.

History as Science

Historians (and others interested in human history, like anthropologists) have been reluctant to accept that 'history' can be studied scientifically. They often argue that history is a collection of singular events, and that attempts to make generalisations, as is regularly done in science, are inappropriate in history. I hope to have shown in this book that when one looks at broader aspects of history, like the five levels of cultural organisation, there are many worthwhile and interesting generalisations to be made. Most of these can be tested, and thus they have a scientific character. It seems that human history can be scientific.

END NOTES

Chapter ONE

1. The research which has led to this scheme was pursued over many years. A preliminary version of it was published in 1991 (D. Collins Human History: an evolutionary view. Clayhanger Books. Tiverton). The scheme in its present form was presented in two recent academic works – Collins 1998 Levels of Culture and Human History; and Collins 2000 The Evolution of Human Culture, both published by Clayhanger Books as above These works are more extensively referenced.

2. For a fuller discussion of the beginning of level I, and the definition of toolmaking, see chapter 3 pages 19 and 20, and Collins 2000 as above.

3. The Mesoric Interlevel between the Paleoric level I and the Neoric level II ends when farming becomes the main basis of subsistence. It supercedes the Paleoric when the transition to farming begins, but there are other developments which also take a society beyond the Paleoric. i.) The beginnings of pastoralism, herding domestic animals. ii.) The beginning of sedentary living, achieved by 'controlling' a food supply based on 'harvesting' wild plants or animals. iii.) Acculturation from any level higher than level I. See Collins 2000 for a more detailed account.

4. This is the Cratoric Interlevel (II/III) which begins, as we shall see in chapter 5, with the appearance of the state; and it ends with the appearance of literacy and level III proper.

5. There are other possible reasons for arguing that a state has transcended the Gramoric, level III, but they are not important in the present context.

6. A more formal account of this general theory will be found in Collins 2000.

7. The use of the terms higher and lower does **not** imply any kind of value judgement; it simply refers to the numbering of the levels from I to II and so on. See, later in this chapter, principle 3 – objectivity.

8. As a matter of fact it also seems to have been impossible for a whole society to move to a **lower** level, and still achieve a stable adaptation. Such 'retro-evolution' does not seem to occur.

9. This is a sub-principle of the general principle of necessary sequence; it could be called 'the impossibility of unassisted culture level by-passing'.

End notes for chapter 1 continued

10. Large areas of Europe away from the mediterranean did not directly experience level III - the Gramoric, (though indirectly some may have been influenced, for example by the phoenicians or the myceneans). Instead they mainly came under greco-roman (technically Alpha-Novaric) influence, while still essentially at level II. Their eventual achievement of the Beta-Novaric sub-level was, however, a prolonged and 'painful' process (involving the so-called 'dark ages'). Evidently a stable 'upward' adaptation under these circumstances is not easy. Similarly japanese culture managed to 'leap-frog' level IV and early level V, but again the process involved major acculturation, and was not achieved without problems and setbacks over a considerable period of time.

11. An example is the Maoris of southern New Zealand, who arrived from other pacific islands with a form of food production, consisting of tropical horticulture. They found that as they moved south of northernmost New Zealand, their form of horticulture would not operate in the colder climates, and they reverted to extensive hunting. In this case, they never achieved a stable adaptation to hunting and gathering, and remained in some form of interlevel between levels I and II. Some sort of collapse of literate states is also common, and this usually results in a society situated intermediate between levels II and III.

12. In such cases, the people will have the characteristics which put them in the interlevel between the two levels in question.

13. However, it is reasonable to expect that having accurate factual knowledge enables administrations to pursue goals in a way which is less likely to seem misguided in retrospect.

14. There are three sub-levels in level I – Primo-Paleoric, Medio-Paleoric and Lepto-Paleoric. There are two sub-levels in level II – Mono-Neoric and Alto-Neoric. There are two sub-levels in level IV – Alpha-Novaric and Beta-Novaric. There are two sub-levels in level V – Pleno-Cenoric and Neo-Cenoric. (There are no subdivisions in level III.) The level I sub-levels are treated briefly in appendix B.

15. A society of level II (the Neoric) which is influenced by a state of level III (the Gramoric) will belong to the Para-Gramoric, and will fall in interlevel II/III. The four interlevels are:- I/II – the Mesoric; II/III – the Cratoric; III/IV – the Proto-Novaric; and IV/V – the Proto-Cenoric.

16. This is the 'hypothetico-deductive' method, advocated most effectively and authoritatively by Sir Karl Popper:- 1959 The Logic of Scientific Discovery, Hutchinson; 1963 Conjectures and Refutations, Routledge; 1972 Objective Knowledge, OUP. For its application to the human sciences see Collins 1973 (in the Explanation of Culture Change, ed. C.Renfrew 1973:53-59 Duckworth), Collins 1998, and Collins 2000.

17. See David Brown 1991 (Human Universals. McGraw-Hill. New York) where the problem of universals is discussed at length and with great insight.

End notes

Chapter TWO

1. Evidence of stone toolmaking is quite common from the period one and a half to two million years ago. But from the earlier time span, of two to two and a half million years ago, it is much rarer. There are perhaps four or five cases that are generally accepted, and more evidence (and better publication of the existing evidence) is needed. The oldest apparent occurrence is from the Hadar-Gona site in Ethiopia, dated at about two and a half million years ago.

2. Unfortunately reliable figures for the size of the meat component do not seem to be available – the figure of two per cent of the food has been quoted.

3. See Richard Wrangham and Dale Peterson (1997 Demonic Males. Bloomsbury, London) who give an extended account of aggression and violence in apes.

4. Achievements of trained chimps in using sign language or touch operated voice synthesizers are not of course indicative of normal behaviour in the natural state.

5. See for example Alison Jolly (1972 The Evolution of Primate Behaviour. Macmillan, New York) who compared chimpanzee thought to the most advanced sub-stage of thinking in the Sensorimotor stage (or stage I) of Jean Piaget's scheme of cognitive development, and she compared lower primate thought to the ('trial and error') sub-stage below this. See chapter 3, note 23.

6. There has unfortunately long been an irrational tendency to 'create' new species and lineages on the slenderest fossil evidence, in flagrant contradiction of one of the most valuable principles of science – that of 'parsimony' or Occam's principle.

7. A more sophisticated measure - the encephalisation quotient of Harry Jerison 1973 (The Evolution of the Brain and Intelligence. Academic Press, New York) gives the following approximate 'EQ' values:- chimpanzees - 2.5; gracilins - 4.7; modern humans - 6.3.

8. As argued in 1970 by Cliff Jolly (Man: NS 5:5-26)

9. These are known as Broca's and Wernicke's areas. They are indicated as present on the inside of skulls from Olduvai (no. 24) and Koobi Fora beside lake Turkana (formerly Rudolf) – skull ER 1470. See Phillip Tobias 1981 (Philos. Trans. of Royal Soc. B 292:43 ff, and Dean Falk 1983 Science 221:1072-4.

10. See Charles Hockett and R.Ascher 1964 (Current Anthropology 5:135-168)

End notes

Chapter THREE
1. In my two recent books (Collins 1998 and 2000), I chose to use the term toolcraft to clarify the important difference between ape 'tool behaviour' and true human toolmaking. The term was first used by nineteenth century anthropologists. For ape tool behaviour, see William McGrew 1992 (Chimpanzee Material Culture. C.U.P.).

2. The 'tool' used in making a tool may be unmodified, modified or manufactured. A tool which has been manufactured is often referred to by archaeologists as an artefact.

3. The definition of culture is notoriously difficult, but a convenient criterion is that true cultural behaviour has both a linguistic and a toolcraft (or artefactual) element. Extending the term to all learned behaviour is unwise.

4. In the 1980s and 1990s, it was claimed that until as late as the time of neanderthal man (say 50,000 years ago), hunting was beyond the capabilities of these stone age tool users, and their ancestors. (This idea even found its way into a number of books.) No sensible arguments were ever offered to support this view, and counter-indications were abundant. With the discovery of a series of long wooden spears from the early old stone age site of Schöningen, dating from long before fifty thousand years ago, this implausible claim has been clearly refuted, and seems to have been dropped.

5. There are a number of cases from the european old stone age, notably the very rich settlements found in the valleys of south west France, and some localities further east in Europe, where sites do seem to have been occupied for all or most of the year, (not necessarily by more than a fraction of the then population). It is currently an open question whether these societies had transcended the bounds of the level I Paleoric proper, but they do seem to have come close to this.

6. The dog sledges of the eskimo are probably a relatively recent phenomenon, only made possible by contact with more advanced asiatic peoples, who bred domestic dogs or huskies. The travoise used by american indians, and pulled by horses, is not known to have a long ancestry back into the hunter stage.

7. An unusually long chain of exchange existed in Queensland. The northern peoples had easy access to sting ray barbs, convenient for use on spears, (but no good source of stone for toolmaking). The southern peoples had easy access to good quality stone for toolmaking, but not to suitable barbs. Thus a chain of exchange was set up.

8. Talk of hunter-gatherers as an 'affluent' society (M. Sahlins 1974 Stone Age Economics. Tavistock, London) seems to confuse their relatively abundant but intermittent leisure with affluence in its correct sense of possessing large quantities of disposable wealth.

End notes for chapter 3

9. Because local or general environmental circumstances can have a considerable effect on population density, we must be careful to compare like with like, and to use large enough areas to cancel out localised anomalies. We can use population data for the same area over several different levels of culture. We can compare different culture levels by using samples from each, matched for a particular kind of environment, or we can use very large areas covering a range of favourable and unfavourable environments, which seem to balance out.

In a typical continent, where unfavourable terrain makes up half or more of the total area, and 'average' and 'favourable' terrain makes up less than half of the total, a density for hunters is typically around 4 or 5 persons per 100 km^2. If we adjust so that the favoured and unfavourable terrain are roughly balanced, the figure rises to about 6 or 7 persons per km^2. The problem is examined in detail in Collins 1998, chapter 3. The figures used here are a digest of a large quantity of relevant data, evaluated in that work (Collins 1998:42-82).

10. The figures used here are from various sources, which will be found in Collins 1998:86-84, and which are analysed in chapter four of that work.

11. It has been claimed that chimps use leaves as wipes, and that these leaves have mildly antiseptic properties.

12. This slowing down and prolonging of the process of maturation is something called by biologists 'neoteny'. There are reasons to think that such a process contributed to the acquisition of a larger brain and improved intellect. See Sir Gavin de Beer 1958 Embryos and Ancestors. O.U.P., and for its relevance to later human evolution D. Collins 1986 Palaeolithic Europe :161-170. Clayhanger Books, Tiverton.

13. Technically this is sometimes referred to as the patrilocal band, related patrilineally. Such a band usually has a name of some sort.

14. See Lawrence Keeley 1991 War before Civilisation. O.U.P.

15. Claims that chimps can be trained to communicate in grammatical english, by pushing buttons on a voice synthesiser, would not alter the fact that in the wild they do not speak, but only make a few grunts and screeches.

16. See Richard Alexander 1989 (The Evolution of the Human Psyche in The Human Revolution eds. P. Mellars and C. Stringer. Edinburgh Univ. Press)

17. This conclusion comes primarily from the ethnographic sample, in which myth is universal. But there are also strong hints of myth in cave art. This does not necessarily mean that myth goes back to the dawn of hunter-gatherers.

18. See Collins 1998, chapter 6 esp. 120ff.

End notes for chapter 3

19. The name 'shaman' comes from the language of the Tungus of Siberia. They were formerly hunters, but have long been herders. Each hunter-gatherer people has its own name for these 'shamans' – for example *karadji* among some australian aborigines, and *angakoq* in the inuit eskimo.

20. Across human history, religion is most conveniently defined as the mythic and ritual complex.

21. The case of Helen Keller is the best known; she later became a government advisor and author.

22. However Piaget himself, to my knowledge, never claimed that particular primitive human levels of culture had thought similar to the earlier stages he identified in the cognitive development of modern children.

23. Piaget's stages of cognitive development have often been set out, but in fact he altered his system several times in a rather confusing way. The following summary of the broad scheme is perhaps the most widely accepted:-

Stage I   SENSORIMOTOR with six substages
Substage 1 - birth to one month; 2 - one to four months; 3 - four to ten months;
4 - ten to twelve months; 5 - twelve to eighteen months; 6 - 18 to 24 months.
[Jolly refers to substage 5 as the trial and error stage, and substage 6 as the stage of deferred imitation and symbolic play.]
Stage II   PRE-OPERATIONAL with two substages
Substage IIa   Pre-Conceptual   two to four years
Substage IIb   Intuitive   four to seven years
Stage III   CONCRETE OPERATIONAL   seven to eleven years;
          Especially associated with a full grasp of 'Conservation'
Stage IV   FORMAL OPERATIONAL   eleven years plus;
          Hypothetico-Deductive reasoning

For a further outline of the scheme, see for example R. McIlveen and R. Gross 1997 (Developmental Psychology. Hodder and Stoughton). For the question of primate thought, see Alison Jolly 1972, esp. pages 306-7 and 319 (The Evolution of Primate Behaviour. Macmillan, New York), and for primitive thought, see C.R.Hallpike 1979 (The Foundations of Primitive Thought. O.U.P.).

24. See J. Piaget 1929 (french original 1926) The Child's Conception of the World. Routledge, London.

25. See Henri Frankfort and colleagues 1949: 12-14   Before Philosophy. Penguin, Harmondsworth.

Chapter FOUR

1. As early as 1834, the swedish professor Sven Nilsson argued that agriculture was a major advance; but the modern idea really stems from V. Gordon Childe, and his concept of the 'neolithic revolution' (in Man Makes Himself 1936 Watts, London).

2. Technically this is here called the Mesoric Interlevel. Also in the same interlevel are various other kinds of society:- Herders or pastoralists who grew no crops and were nomadic; Hunter-gatherers who found wild food sources which were so abundant, that they were able to adopt settled living on the basis of this 'wild harvesting'. The Mesoric interlevel also includes various kinds of acculturated hunter-gatherers, some living in symbiosis with farmers. The section of the Mesoric which is specifically transitional to agriculture is called Trans-Mesoric (see Collins 1998 and Collins 2000).

3. See Collins 1998 chapter 3. While for hunters a typical density was around 0.06 persons per km^2, it was closer to 6 or 7 persons per km^2 for tribal farmers. The density of population in tribal chiefdoms (of the Alto-Neoric) was regularly a little higher. For premature mortality and life expectancy the figures are all from Collins 1998 chapter 4.

4. Metals are virtually unknown among the tribal farmers of the americas, outside the andean area. Iron only spread in eurasia after iron smelting was developed by the Hittites, about 1800 to 1100 B.C.

5. There is a claim for the use of textiles over twenty thousand years ago, at a site in Czechoslovakia. Like the peoples of the Dordogne area, these 'hunters' may possibly have passed beyond the Paleoric level proper into the Mesoric interlevel.

6. This is why the farming tribe is often referred to as the 'segmentary' tribe. It always has stronger cohesion in the smallest segments, and is weakest in the largest.

7. An exception is 'black' Africa, where slavery is common in the simple tribal (Mono-Neoric) peoples, and near universal in the tribal chiefdoms (of the Alto-Neoric).

8. The topic of numeracy was dealt with in more detail in Collins 1998, chapter 5. (The presence of a 5-20 counting system in some eskimo peoples is almost certainly a recent derivation from east Asia – where this system is common. It 'overlays' a two-count, which remained quite widespread among the eskimos.)

9. As explained in Collins 1998:185, the Fuegians of southernmost South America have several mythic traits which are typical in tribal farmers, and this is may be due to descent from or contact with farmers.

10. There is also a common distinction between a 'day' witch and a 'night' witch!

End notes for chapter 4 continued

11. Examples are 'auspices' (birds), 'haruspices' (entrails), 'scapulomancy' (cracks in bones or scapulae), 'geomancy' (thrown handfuls of earth) and 'dice' (often a calcaneum bone).

12. A good example is some elementary 'topology' (such as notions of proximity, separation, continuity and ordering).

Chapter FIVE

1. A useful source on the origin of the state is Lawrence Krader 1968 (The Formation of the state. Prentice-Hall, Englewood Cliffs, New Jersey). The appearance of the state marks the end of level II – the Neoric.

2. If the 'chief' had supreme power, he would by definition be a monarch, and the 'tribe' would become a state.

3. See Collins 2000:125-6.

4. The first chinese dynasty (the Shang) certainly had numerous slaves, and slavery continued in subsequent dynasties. It has been claimed that the later dynasties had fewer slaves, and that the institution died out in these later dynasties.

5. The lower or Mono-Neoric sub-level by definition has no formal social classes, but slaves were sometimes held in such tribes which otherwise lacked any form of stratification. The higher sub-level or Alto-Neoric was already ranked in some way, but did not apparently have a formal class system. Slaves, however, were commoner, and the egalitarian ethos has disappeared.

6. See Collins 1998 chapter 4.

7. That is to say , in similar environments, or best of all in the same region. See Collins 1998, chapter 3 and references.

8. See Karl Wittfogel 1957 (Oriental Despotism. Yale U.P., New Haven)

9. But the polynesians accomplished amazing voyages, in relatively small boats.

10. The shaduf consists of a horizontal pole with a water bucket on one end, and a counterweight on the other end; it is mounted and hinged on an upright pole, for easy transfer of water from a channel to an irrigation system. The sakhia is a sophicated device, powered by a beast turning a wheel, which rotates a vertically mounted wheel with buckets on it. It can thus raise water for irrigation without human effort.

11. According to a model advanced by Sir Karl Popper, there were three 'worlds':-
The world of physical states (which goes back to the origins of the physical cosmos); The world of mental or emotional states (which begins with 'sentient' animals); and thirdly the world of 'objective' contents of thought. The latter can only come into existence with language, but assumed much greater importance with the advent of writing.

End notes

Chapter SIX

1. The date of invention of the true alphabet is not accurately known. It could be almost anywhere in the period 700 to 1000 B.C. Nor is the place known, but an interesting case has been made out for Al Mina, a predominantly greek entrepôt, on the east mediterranean coast near the border of Syria and Turkey, where greeks traded with phoenicians. The consonantal script (perhaps best called by its semitic name – aleph-beth) was used widely in the levant, but it was almost certainly from the phoenician/canaanite people that the greeks borrowed it. Originally all the letters were 'capitals'. (Lower case letters were only introduced in post-classical times).

2. It is known that the mycenean greeks, of a period a few centuries before this, used a syllabic script (linear B), which basically consisted of a sign for a 'consonant with a vowel following it' (see John Chadwick 1987 Linear B.   British Museum Publications, London). They used the same five vowels which later greeks employed, and one may speculate that the vowels, introduced when the greeks adapted the semitic script, were chosen because they had survived in a greek writing tradition.

3. Formal logic was not used until somewhat later, by Aristotle, for example.

4. See Frankfort et al 1949, already quoted in the previous chapter; and also Robin Horton 1993   Patterns of Thought in Africa and the West. C.U.P.

5. We need to remember that practical tests and experiments were rare at this level, and did not become common until the age of empiricism, beginning during the scientific revolution of 1500 to 1700 A.D.

6. It is true that a secular view of the world was not encouraged by much of medieval christianity, but a rational and secular approach did in fact survive through this time. Indeed William of Occam was the inventor of the key scientific principle of 'parsimony' – (Entia non sunt multiplicanda, praeter necessitatem, or always choose the simplest explanation that is possible and sufficient.)

7. There is of course the brief episode in egyptian history when the 'heretic' pharaoh Akhenaten established a monotheistic sun worship, but this did not thrive. Nor is it clear if there was any connection between this and the story of Moses in Egypt. Monotheistic Judaism may not have been fully established until long after 1000 B.C.

8. Some authorities hold that chinese circular metal coins were an independent invention in China, but this is debatable.

9. It is interesting that the phoenicians were not only among the first to adopt ironworking; they also 'presaged' the greeks in other fields, such as their aleph-beth script, in long distance voyaging, and in long distance pioneer trading.

10. Estimates will be found in Collins 1998 chapters 3 and 4.

End notes for chapter 6 continued

11. There are some hints that mycenean civilisation was not entirely typical of this level. For example Kontorlis 1985:35 (Mycenean Civilisation. Kontorli, Athens) says 'as appears from the translation of the linear B tablets, at the head of the common classes was the 'wanax', absolute monarch, with all powers centred in himself.' This is completely typical of the Gramoric. Later he adds 'the wanax was probably surrounded by a council of land-holding nobles.' This suggests some movement in the direction which greek society later took in the Novaric level. Wealth seems to have been based on trade, and hydraulic projects have not so far been identified.

12. Tyranny or tyrants meant to the greeks usurping rulers, who had no legitimate right, by succession for example, to rule. The very usage of the term by all, including those who disliked 'democracy', is indicative of a change in collective thinking from the level III acceptance of autocratic monarchy.

13. The curia and comitia were various ancient kinds of assembly of some or all of the classes of the roman people. The comitia were originally based partly on tribal membership.

14. Four 'mathematical' skills made up the quadrivium – arithmetic, geometry, astronomy and music. Together with the trivium, they made up the 'seven liberal arts'.

15. See Lynn White 1964 Medieval technology and social change. O.U.P. – chapter 1 for the stirrup, and chapter 2 for the plough and iron technology.

Chapter SEVEN

1. Level V (the Cenoric) starts, as we shall see, with the industrial revolution at about 1700 A.D. Its second sub-level (the Neo-Cenoric) starts around 1900 A.D. No date for the end of the Cenoric is suggested here. This is because any further sub-levels, levels or interlevels (which will presumably be needed) with their definition and starting dates will be best fixed with the benefit of hindsight. Some boundary between 1980 and 2020 A.D. seems likely.
    It is important to emphasise that neither the Cenoric, nor any previous level is defined by 'dates'. The levels are defined by culture features. Many parts of the globe did not move into the Cenoric around 1700, or even 1850 A.D. Nor did they move into the Neo-Cenoric around 1900 A.D. Large areas of the world remain incompletely adapted to the new level, and have only been acculturated in various degrees.

2. In the system of levels, the dawn of the scientific revolution marks the transition from the Novaric level to the Proto-Cenoric interlevel. The culmination of the scientific revolution, along with the industrial revolution, mark the end of the Proto-Cenoric and the start of the Cenoric proper.

3. The core countries or regions, involved by 1700 include Britain, France, the low countries, Germany with 'mitteleuropa' and Italy, as well as southern Scandinavia.

End notes for chapter 7 continued

4. For all his genius, Leonardo da Vinci was a 'renaissance man' rather than a genuine scientist. He may be seen as the herald of the scientific revolution, but on current evidence, there is no reason to think that he started it.

5. This was the work of Abraham Darby ('the first'). At the same time, the steam engine was being developed by Thomas Savery (1698) and especially by Thomas Newcomen (1706). Some seventy years were to pass before James Watt and his associates produced a really efficient steam power engine.

6. Japan is one of the few exceptions, but there had been some western contact here.

7. See Collins 1998, chapter 4.

8. This applies only to the core Neo-Cenoric states, which have been widely imitated elsewhere. Democratic rule has had notable lapses.

9. My own view is that by far the most important contribution has been the clarification by Sir Karl Popper of the logic behind scientific research, (using Tarski's refined concept of factual truth). It has been summed up as:- Initial Problem Situation $\rightarrow$ Tentative Theory $\rightarrow$ Error Elimination $\rightarrow$ New Problem Situation, or $P^1 \rightarrow$ $TT \rightarrow EE \rightarrow P^2$) - a continuous process of improvement of the closeness to the truth of our conceptions.

10. As Einstein put it, 'Religion without science is blind; and Science without religion is lame'.

11. In the twentieth century, with the enrolment into the Cenoric of countries like Japan and Israel, and some near secular states, the situation has changed somewhat.

12. Usually the participants in these revivals are not well informed on the details of the originals, and are happy to make it up as they go along. In this way, they are not very far from those originals.

13. The principle mover in this cause was William Wilberforce, whose legislation was adopted in 1807. Apparently Denmark introduced laws to this effect slightly earlier.

Chapter EIGHT
1. Normally the supporting capacity provided by the technique of food acquisition is directly related to the population density. But in twentieth century, advanced level V countries, this correlation is no longer valid. Advanced western countries have regularly increased the supporting capacity of their land, but not increased their (already large) populations to the same degree. During the preceding chapters, we have noted the increased densities of population which (until the twentieth century) have reflected increasing food production.

2. Normally Gross National Product is divided by the number of people in the state, giving a *per capita* value, which is a broad indicator of wealth.

APPENDIX A

The 'sample' of pre-literate and literate peoples

Level I (the Paleoric hunter-gatherers)

The most regularly useful part of the sample consists of four peoples:- the australian aborigines, with perhaps 600 paleo-tribes; the inuit or eskimo with over 100 paleo-tribes; the andaman islanders with about a dozen paleo-tribes; and the malay peninsula negritos or semang with a similar number of paleo-tribes. [As pointed out in the next appendix – B, the tasmanian aborigines are plausible representatives of the 'earlier' Medio-Paleoric sub-level, and thus of special potential interest.]

The next most useful group includes the american 'indians' of the subarctic region of north america with at least 30 paleo-tribes; the 'Fuegian' peoples of southernmost south america, with only a few known paleo-tribes; and the San 'bushmen' of the Kalahari and adjacent southern african area. (These latter include several paleo-tribes with different languages, but problems of acculturation are particularly serious in this case.)

More problematic are:- the congo pygmies, who live in the rainforest of central africa, mainly in symbiosis with farmers; and the siberian hunters of whom only two peoples out of a formerly much larger number survived long enough for any observations on them to be made by anthropologists. The Hadza of east africa and the Tasaday of the philippines have to be used in the sample only with great caution.

Level II (the Neoric tribal farmers)

Africa provides the largest sample. On figures provided by George Murdock (1959), there are some 237 simple tribes and 194 tribal chiefdoms in the sample. The great majority are negro peoples or related nilotic negroids. In north east africa there are a few caucasoid farming tribes.

A second useful area is Oceania. This includes New Guinea and Melanesia, as well as polynesian and micronesian peoples spread over a wide area from Easter island to New Zealand and to Hawaii. There is some good evidence from the 'pueblo' peoples of the southwestern U.S.A., and from the araucanians of Chile and some other south american peoples. The best asian evidence is from indonesia, especially Borneo. No tribal farmers survived in Europe down to recent times.

Level III (the Gramoric archaic literates states)

The best evidence for these comes from Mesopotamian civilisations, Egyptian civilisation, Chinese civilisation, Japanese civilisation, and in Meso-america, the Maya and the Aztecs.

More problematic for various reasons are Mycenean civilisation, Hittite civilisation, Levantine civilisations (Ebla, Ugarit, Byblos and Canaan), Persian civilisations, Aryan Indian civilisation, Ethiopic and Khmer civilisations. In the case of Minoan (pre-Mycenean) Crete and the Harappan civilisation of the Indus basin, the scripts cannot yet be read.

Level IV (the Novaric, greco-roman and medieval states)

The main sources for the earlier Novaric are greek hellenic and hellenistic civilisation and roman civilisation. For the later Novaric, medieval western christendom is the core area, but some neighbours made important contributions. For example, islamic civilisation was responsible for bringing the hindu system of numerals to the west.

Level V (the Cenoric, industrial and science-based civilisations)

In the Proto-Cenoric, Italy was the centre of the renaissance, and the iberians were the main force in world colonisation. But in the early Cenoric proper, there was a core of five main 'players' – France, Germany (with 'mitteleuropa'), Italy, Britain and the low countries. Scandinavia and parts of central europe were also significant. Later, countries like the U.S.A., Canada, Australia and New Zealand, and Japan became important players also.

G.P.Murcock 1959 Africa: its peoples and their culture. McGraw-Hill. New York

APPENDIX B

The subdivisions of level I (the Paleoric hunter-gatherers)

The three sub-levels proposed here (Primo-Paleoric, Medio-Paleoric and Lepto-Paleoric) are broadly similar to the three divisions used by many archaeologists for Europe and adjacent areas – namely Lower Palaeolithic, Middle Palaeolithic and Upper Palaeolithic. (The latter have little consistent definition, and what they have – for example that the Upper Palaeolithic ends at the same time as the last ice age, irrespective of culture features – is often unsatisfactory and unhelpful.)

The first sub-level has only simple stone tools, of which so-called handaxes and chopping tools are perhaps the most widespread. There is little doubt that these humans had speech, and were hunters and gatherers, who derived a significant portion of their diet from meat. I would suggest that these early humans had all the main features of level I.

The second sub-level (Medio-Paleoric) is recognised in the archaeological record by the presence of 'flake tools'. These include flakes of a predetermined shape removed by a single blow from specially prepared cores; (this is often called the Levallois technique). Although this has sometimes been seen as a sufficient definition of the start of middle palaeolithic, it is inadequate; even late in the 'middle palaeolithic', such tools are regularly absent. One must also include flake tools, which consist of a stone flake that has been 'retouched' or trimmed by further small flake removal to alter its shape or its working edge. So-called sidescrapers are very typical.

This new stone toolworking technique seems first to appear more than a quarter of a million years ago, but less than half a million. At around the same time, the occupation of cave mouths and rockshelters seems to begin, and hearths are found. Although fire was almost certainly used in the first sub-level, (mainly in its later part), it seems that the ability to make fire at will is new to this second sub-level. Regular firemaking probably made it possible for humans to eject cave dwelling predators, and to occupy the caves themselves.

The third sub-level (the Lepto-Paleoric) seems to have stone toolmaking, which regularly includes a greater variety of more standardised tool types, and a tendency to slender, miniaturised tools. Distinctive missile tips of stone or bone are also now common, and distinctive bone tool types are for the first time typically found, though not necessarily universal in the new level. The types of tool which characterise this phase vary greatly from region to region. A concentration on narrow blades is typical of most of Europe and adjacent areas, but elsewhere the situation can be very different.

In addition, where the evidence is good enough to judge, it seems that the pace of change in the Lepto-Paleoric is considerably faster than it was in the preceding sub-levels, where no obvious culture change is detectable over tens or even hundreds of thousands of years. In the third sub-level, as in later levels, culture change is detectable in less than ten thousand years, often in one or two thousand years. In the Lepto-Paleoric we find musical instruments for the first time, and also representational art, though the latter is sometimes absent. For a more detailed treatment of the archaeological evidence, see Collins 1986 and 1976.

The first appearance of the Lepto-Paleoric seems to be in the order of forty five thousand years ago. (The problem is complicated by lack of agreement on a clear and general definition of what constitutes the new sub-level, and disagreement on whether it was introduced by a wave of new invaders or not.) According to one view, it is earliest in south east and central Europe, and a bit later in western Europe and the near east. As we note below, it seems to be much later in Australasia.

There is little doubt that most surviving hunter-gatherers, known to ethnography, belong or belonged to the third sub-level. This seems to be true of of the aborigines of the australian mainland, the eskimos, and the San bushmen for example. However in the case of the Tasmanian aborigines, who became culturally extinct in the nineteenth century, there is no indication that they had reached the Lepto-Paleoric sub-level, and on available evidence they seem to fall in the preceding sub-level. The whole question of the nature and date of this transition away from Europe tends to be more obscure, but it seems that on the australian mainland the analogous transition occurred some five to seven thousand years ago, near the middle of the post-glacial or 'holocene' geological phase. This transition does not seem to occur at all in Tasmania, where the earlier sub-level apparently survived down to recent times, in isolation from the mainland. The prima facie case for this is strong, but the matter is controversial.

D.Collins 1976 The Human Revolution. Phaidon. Oxford

D.Collins 1986 Palaeolithic Europe. Clayhanger. Tiverton

INDEX